# art / shop / eat
# MILAN

Paul Blanchard

Via Certosa

Via

Via Ugo Bassi

Via Cenisio

Staz. Porta
Garibaldi F.S.

Corso

Via

Via Ceresio

Viale Crispi Bastioni di Po

Bastioni
di P.ta Volta

Via
Alcunio

Viale

Via

Sempione

P.za
VI Febbraio

pp. 52-53

Via
Legnano

P.za
Sempione

Parco

Sempione

pp. 8-9

Via Pontaccio Via Fa

Pinacoteca
di Brera

Via
Buonarroti

Via

Via

Ariosto

pp. 98-99

Castello Sforzesco

Via Bramante

Staz. Ferr. Nord

Museo Po
Pezz

Corso

Vercelli

Foro

Via Dante

Santa Maria
delle Grazie

Via Carducci

Magenta

Piazza
Cordusio

The Duo

Washington

Viale di Porta Vercellina

Corso

Civiche Raccolte
Archeologiche
e Numismatiche

Via
G.

pp. 122-123

Sant'Ambrogio

Via Torino

Palazz
Real

Museo Nazionale
di Scienza e Tecnologia

Via Olona

Via Edmondo de

Viale

Corso

Italia

Via

Foppa

Amicis

Via

Ticinese

Via
Martino

delle Armi

Via S.

Corso

Viale
Misurata

Via

Vincenzo

Paramino

Via

Corso Genova

Corso di Porta

P.za
Napoli

2

Via Troya

C. Colombo

Viale G. D'Annunzio

Staz. di Genova

di

Ticinese

Porta

P.le
XXIV Maggio

V.le
Gian Galeazzo

Corso
Gottardo

Viale

Rina

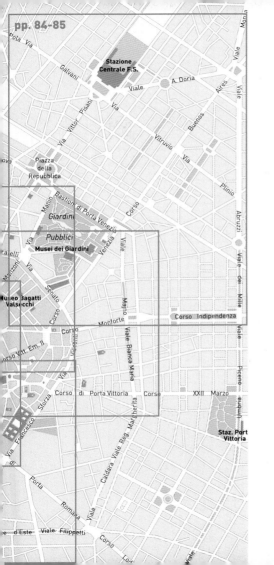

Stazione
Centrale F.S.

Piazza
della
Repubblica

Giardini

Pubblici

Musei dei Giardini

Museo Bagatti
Valsecchi

Corso Indipendenza

Staz. Port
Vittoria

Corso di Porta Vittoria

Corso Vitt. Em. II

XXII Marzo

CITY OVERVIEW

3

# The City Centre

# Brera

# Porta Venezia

# Sant'Ambrogio

# Pinacoteca Ambrosiana

# introduction

Once the major military capial of the Roman empire, Milan is now a bustling town known for fashion and a leisurely urban lifestyle. The city's fame is not just based on Prada; the splendid façade and brilliant stained glass of the Duomo and the early Christian basilicas like Sant'Ambrogio bear witness to the development of the city as a major cultural centre. The Renaissance brought new ideas to Milan, and— luckily for the city—it brought Leonardo da Vinci, too, who sought patronage at the court of the ruling Sforza family and painted his *Last Supper* for the church of Santa Maria delle Grazie.

Over time Milan developed outwards, but where once there were *navigli* (canals) or *bastioni* (fortifications), now there are wide boulevards. The vast Brera Gallery, one of Europe's best art museums, is here, as is the small but wonderful Ambrosiana Gallery.

The Milan of today is lively and cosmopolitan—Milan's Fashion Week is one of the industry's top events. But there's a quieter side to Milan, too. There's no better way to relax than to sit outside and people-watch while sipping a glass of another local name made big: Campari.

The five main chapters of art/shop/eat Milan show you the best of every section of the city. The planning section will help you negotiate Milan's swift and simple metro system, while the entertainment chapter lists musical venues, including the brilliant Scala opera house, graced by so many of the world's finest voices. The glossary provides background on the influential artists whose work hangs in the galleries of Milan.

# THE CITY CENTRE

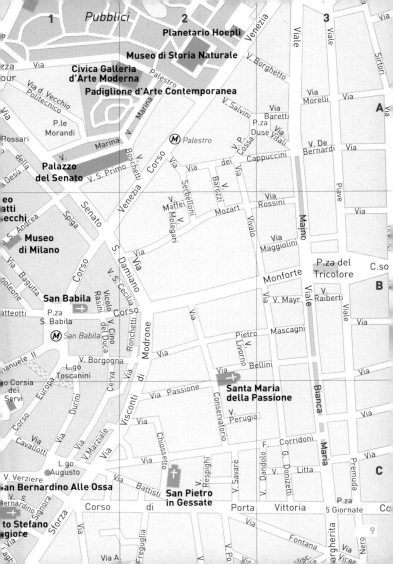

Modern Milan is in essence a Roman and medieval town, and if you look at a map you can see the ghost of old Milan in the kernel of the city centre. There was a Roman forum on the site of Piazza San Sepolcro and the medieval seat of government stood where the Palazzo Reale is today—right next to the splendid bulk of the Duomo, the city's religious centre. The centre also holds most of the shopping: flagship stores of top designers line the streets around via Montenapoleone; the glass ceiling of the elegant Galleria Vittorio Emanuele II shelters boutiques and cafés; the corso from the Duomo to San Babila has every major chain.

# The Duomo

| | |
|---|---|
| **OPEN** | The *Duomo* is open every day, 7 am–7 pm; *Roof*, 9 am–5.45 pm, February–November, and 9 am–4.45 pm, December–January. *Battistero di San Giovanni*, every day, 9.45 am–12.45 pm and 2 pm–5.45 pm. Tickets at the bookshop. |
| **CLOSED** | *Roof* 1/1, 25/4, 1/5, 25/12 |
| **CHARGES** | Entrance to the *Duomo* is free. *Roof* €3.50 (stairs) or €5.00 (lift); cumulative ticked for roof plus *Museo del Duomo* €7.00; *Battistero di San Giovanni* €1.50 |
| **GUIDED VISITS** | Audio guides available |
| **DISABLED ACCESS** | Yes (ask at bookshop) |
| **SERVICES** | Bookshop inside the cathedral |
| **TELEPHONE** | 02 7202 2656 |
| **WEB** | www.duomomilano.com |
| **MAIN ENTRANCE** | *Cathedral*, left door of the façade; *Roof* stairs, south transept, near the Medici tomb; *Lift*, entered from outside the north or south transept. |
| **GETTING THERE** | M1 or M3 to Duomo; tram 2, 3, 4, 12, 14, 15, 23, 24 or 27; bus 60 or 65 |

## HIGHLIGHTS
**Architecture and decoration**

Exterior and
interior

**The climb to the top**

Roof

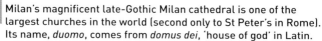

Milan's magnificent late-Gothic Milan cathedral is one of the
largest churches in the world (second only to St Peter's in Rome).
Its name, *duomo*, comes from *domus dei*, 'house of god' in Latin.

This complicated and fascinating structure, the only Gothic
cathedral in Italy, took generations to complete. It was begun in
1386 under Milanese ruler Gian Galeazzo Visconti, who presented
the building committee with a marble quarry at Candoglia that
still belongs to the cathedral chapter. The design is attributed to
Lombard masters, who were assisted by French, German and
Flemish craftsmen.

In 1567 Archbishop Charles Borromeo appointed Pellegrino
Tibaldi as architect. The tower over the crossing was completed
in 1762, and the statue of the Virgin placed on its summit in 1774.
The façade, begun in the 17th C, was completed in 1805.

## EXTERIOR
The façade was begun by **Pellegrino Tibaldi** in the 16th C to a
Classical design but was considerably altered by Carlo Buzzi
(1645) and Francesco Castelli, who adopted a Gothic-revival style.
It was completed in 1805 using Buzzi's design. The doors date
from 1906, 1948, 1950, and 1960.

## INTERIOR
The huge cruciform interior, with double-aisled nave, single-
aisled transepts and a pentagonal apse, has a forest of 52 tall
columns, most of which bear sculpture figures in canopied niches
instead of capitals. The splendid effect is heightened by the
stained glass of the windows and the Classical pavement by
Tibaldi.

# THE DUOMO

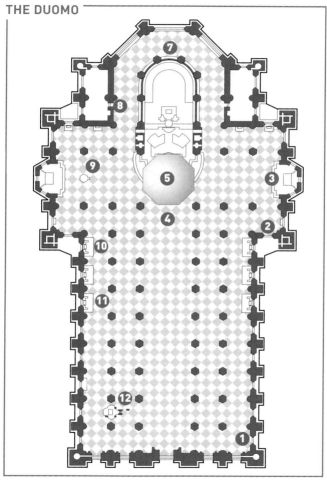

Start your visit in the south aisle. Above the plain granite **sarcophagus of Archbishop Aribert** (d. 1045) **[1]** is a stained-glass window by Cristoforo de' Mottis (1473–77). The next three windows have 16th-C glass, followed by one (1470–75) that shows the influence of Vincenzo Foppa. The glass above the sixth altar is by Nicolò da Varallo (1480–89).

In the south transept is the **monument to Gian Giacomo Medici [2]**, with bronze statues, by Leone Leoni (1560–63). The stained glass in the two transept windows is by Corrado de' Mocchis (1554–64). In the transept apse is the monumental **altar of San Giovanni Bono** (1763) **[3]**. On the altar with a marble relief by **Bambaia** is a statue (right) of *St Catherine*, by

The Resurrection in stained glass

Cristoforo Lombardo. The disturbing statue of *St Bartholomew* flayed and carrying his skin is by Marco d'Agrate (1562).

On the impressive tower over the crossing are **medallions with 15th-C busts of the Doctors of the Church [4]**. The **presbytery [5]** (usually open to worshippers only) was designed by Pellegrino Tibaldi (1567). It contains two pulpits (supported by bronze figures by **Francesco Brambilla**) and a large bronze ciborium, also by Tibaldi.

The **crypt [6]**, decorated with stucco reliefs by Galeazzo Alessi and Tibaldi, contains the richly robed body of St Charles Borromeo, the leading spirit of the Catholic Counter-Reformation, made Cardinal Archbishop of Milan in 1560 and canonised in 1610. The **ambulatory [7]** is separated from the choir by a beautiful marble screen designed by Tibaldi (1567). The Gothic **sacristy** door dates from 1389 **[8]**; the sacristy contains a statue of Christ at the column by Cristoforo Solari.

In the middle of the north transept is the **Trivulzio candelabrum [9]**, a seven-branched bronze candlestick nearly 5 m high, of French or German workmanship and dating from the 13th or 14th C. The stained-glass window above the sculptured altarpiece of the Crucifix (1605) is by Nicolò da Varallo (1479).

In the north aisle, the **eighth altarpiece i**s by Federico Barocci **[10]**. The next four stained-glass windows date from the 16th C. On the sixth altar is the **crucifix carried by St Charles Borromeo [11]** during the plague of 1576; at the third altar, **the tomb of three archbishops of the Arcimboldi family [12]**, attributed to Galeazzo Alessi. Opposite is the font, a **porphyry urn [13]** thought to date from Roman times, covered with a canopy by Tibaldi.

The **excavations** beneath the church are entered from the west end. Here is the 4th-C octagonal baptistery where St Ambrose baptised St Augustine in 387; remains of the basilica of Santa Tecla (begun in the 4th C); and Roman baths of the 1st C BC.

## THE ROOF

The ascent to the roof provides a superb view of the sculptural detail of the exterior. The entrance is a small door in the corner of the south transept, near the Medici tomb. One hundred and fifty-eight steps lead up to the roof of the transept, from which you can see numerous pinnacles and flying buttresses. From the walkways across the roof you can examine the details of the carvings, and beyond are magnificent views of the city. The Carelli spire, the oldest pinnacle, is at the angle facing the Corso.

The Duomo in Numbers

*Length* 158 m

*Height from the interior pavement to the head of the Madoninnina* 108.5 m

*Width of the facade* 67.9 m

*Outer surface area* Approx. 12,000 m2

*Interior surface area* Approx. 800 m2

*Number of sculptures inside and out* Approx. 3,400

*Stained glass* 1,700 m2, containing 3,600 figures

From above the west front it is possible to walk along the spine of the nave roof to the base of the crossing, by Amadeo (1490–1500), who also planned the four turrets but finished only the one at the northeast angle. Stairs lead up from the southwest turret to the platform of the crossing. From here another staircase, in the northeast turret, ascends to the topmost gallery at the base of the central spire. This is surmounted by the *Madonnina*, a statue of gilded copper nearly 4 m high. From here there is a magnificent view of the city, the Lombard plain, the Alps from Monte Viso to the Ortler (with the prominent peaks of the Matterhorn and Monte Rosa) and the Apennines.

# Palazzo Reale
## MUSEO DEL DUOMO, MUSEO DELLA REGGIA AND CIVICO MUSEO D'ARTE CONTEMPORANEA

| | |
|---|---|
| OPEN | The Museo del Duomo is open 9.30 am–12.30 pm and 3 pm–6 pm, Tues-Sun. The Museo della Reggia and the Civico Museo d'Arte Contemporanea open in 2006. |
| CLOSED | Museo del Duomo Mon, 1/1, Easter Sunday, 25/4, 1/5, 25/12 |
| CHARGES | Regular admission to the Museo del Duomo €6; seniors and students €2.58 |
| GUIDED VISITS | Museo del Duomo For talks and guided visits, contact Opera d'Arte at 02 6900 0579. |
| DISABLED ACCESS | Yes (ask at Reception) |
| TELEPHONE | Museo della Reggia 02 875672 Museo del Duomo 02 7202 2656 Civico Museo di Arte Contemporanea 02 8646 3054 |
| WEB | Museo del Duomo www.duomomilano.com |
| MAIN ENTRANCE | Museo della Reggia and Civico Museo d'Arte Contemporanea, Piazza del Duomo 12 Museo del Duomo, Piazza del Duomo 14 |
| GETTING THERE | M1 or M3 to Duomo; tram 2, 3, 4, 12, 14, 15, 23, 24 or 27; bus 60 or 65 |

## HIGHLIGHTS
Sculpture, painting, stained glass, tapestries and liturgical objects from the Gothic to the early Modern age, including Tintoretto's *Infant Christ Among the Doctors*

Museo del Duomo

The former Royal Palace of Milan stands to the south of the cathedral, on the site of the 13th-C town hall. The origins of the palace go back to the Middle Ages, when it was home to the city's rulers, the Torriani, Visconti and Sforza. In the 18th C, Maria Theresa of Austria invited the greatest architects of the time to take part in a competition, the winner to rebuild and redecorate the palace with gold leaf and stucco. Vanvitelli, von Pacassi, Bibiena and Piermarini were the finalists, and the latter won with a design that made extensive use of the pre-existing buildings. Both Napoleon and Vittorio Emanuele of Savoy later lived there. It was heavily bombed in 1943: the Sala delle Cariatidi was left roofless, the fresco by Francesco Hayez that decorated it was lost, and many other works were damaged beyond repair.

## MUSEO DELLA REGGIA
Restoration has proceeded almost continuously since the 1980s. When work is completed, in 2006, the fourteen monumental rooms on the first floor will make up the Museo della Reggia, a sumptuous showcase of historic architecture and urban design, and a prestigious setting for temporary exhibitions.

## MUSEO DEL DUOMO
Opposite the south transept of the cathedral is the entrance to the Museo del Duomo. The collection, arranged in twenty rooms on the ground floor, contains works removed from the duomo for safekeeping or brought from the repository of the Veneranda Fabbrica, the organization that has been in charge of the cathedral since 1386. The visit unfolds chronologically, telling the story of the cathedral's construction and offering a glimpse of religious and artistic life in Milan from the 14th C to the present day.

Highlights include an early work by **Jacopo Tintoretto**, *The Infant*

*Christ among the Doctors*, and a splendid wooden model of the duomo constructed in 1519.

## CIVICO MUSEO D'ARTE CONTEMPORANEA

Restoration work is underway on the second-floor Civico Museo d'Arte Contemporanea; the new installation, designed by venerable architectural firm **BBPR** (Banfi, Belgiojoso, Peresutti and Rogers, creators of the 1957 Torre Velasca), will be ready in autumn 2006. It will include the adjacent Arengario (see below).

### THE MUSEUM OF THE TWENTIETH CENTURY

Milan has been showering the art press with news of its new Museum of the Twentieth Century, which is slated to open in 2006 in the Arengario, a beautiful modern building (1939–56) at the corner of Piazza del Duomo and Via Marconi. The building was designed by Giovanni Muzio and decorated with reliefs by Arturo Martini, and will be reworked by local architect Italo Rota, who plans a spiralling gallery to fill the angular space. When it opens, it is expected to be one of Europe's most ambitious contemporary art galleries.

# Museo Poldi Pezzoli

| | |
|---|---|
| **OPEN** | The museum is open 10 am–6 pm, Tues–Sun. |
| **CLOSED** | Mon, 1/1, Easter Sunday, 25/4, 1/5, 15/8, 1/11, 8/12, 25/12, 26/12 |
| **CHARGES** | Regular admission €6; under 18 and over 60 €4 |
| **GUIDED VISITS** | Audio tours available; guided visits by appointment at 02 794 889 or 02 796 334 |
| **DISABLED ACCESS** | Yes (ask at Reception) |
| **SERVICES** | Bookshop |
| **TELEPHONE** | 02 794 889 |
| **WEB** | www.museopoldipezzoli.it |
| **MAIN ENTRANCE** | Via Manzoni 12 |
| **GETTING THERE** | M1 to Duomo, M3 to Montenapoleone; tram 1, 2; bus 61, 94 |

## HIGHLIGHTS

| | |
|---|---|
| **Paintings by Andrea Mantegna, Giovanni Bellini, Sandro Botticelli, Piero della Francesca and Antionio Pollaiolo** | Salone Dorato |
| **Décor; *Artemesia*, attributed to Luca Signorelli** | Sala Nera |
| **Paintings by Francesco Guardi, Rosalba Carriera and Giambattista Tiepolo** | Sala del Settecento Veneto |
| **Portable altar by Mariotto Albertinelli** | Sala del Perugino |
| **16th-C Persian carpet with hunting scenes** | Sala dell'Affresco |

The Museo Poldi Pezzoli was once the private residence of Gian Giacomo Poldi Pezzoli, a Milanese aristocrat and patron of the arts. He was the son of Rosina Trivulzio and Giuseppe Poldi, whose families were also known for their generous support of the arts. He bequeathed his art collection and 16th-C townhouse to the city in 1879 and it opened to the public in 1881.

Gian Giacomo's collection, acquired between 1846 and 1879, reflects the eclectic tastes of his time: there are works from various regional schools of painting, small paintings, rarities and objets d'art—books, Murano glass, enamels, gold, carpets, tapestries, fabrics and ceramics.

In the *entrance hall* with the ticket office is a portrait of Poldi Pezzoli by Italy's foremost Romantic painter, **Francesco Hayez**. A elliptical staircase, with a baroque fountain and landscapes by **Alessandro Magnasco**, ascends to the main picture gallery on the first floor. To the left are the three little *Salette dei Lombardi*, with *Madonnas* by **Vincenzo Foppa** and **Ambrogio Bergognone**; a portrait by Foppa; *The Rest on the Flight* (with a charming landscape) by **Andrea Solario**; a *Madonna* by **Boltraffio**; and works by **Luini** and the Lombard school.

Beyond the vestibule is the *Sala degli Stranieri* (or antechamber) with paintings by **Cranach**, including portraits of Luther and his wife.

The *Salone Dorato* has the masterpieces of the collection: a *Madonna and Child* and *Portrait of a Man* by **Andrea Mantegna**; a *Pietà* by **Giovanni Bellini**; a *Pietà* and a *Virgin and the Child* by **Botticelli** (see picture opposite); *St Nicholas of Tolentino* by **Piero della Francesca**; and a famous *Portrait of a Lady* by **Antonio Pollaiolo** or his brother Piero.

Beyond the Salone Dorato is the *Sala Nera*, named from its decoration (partly preserved) in ivory and ebony. The beautiful painting of *Artemisia* is attributed to the '**Maestro di Griselda**', whom recent scholars have tentatively identified as Luca Signorelli.

The *Sala dei Vetri Antichi di Murano* contains 17th–19th-C miniatures as well as examples of glass from Murano. The *Sala del Palma*, with a portrait of a courtesan by **Palma il Vecchio** and a small painting by Giovanni Battista Moroni, is entered from the Sala Nera. Also displayed here is the Portaluppi collection of some 200 sundials of the 16th–19th C.

In one of the two *Sale Trivulzio* are interesting Islamic bronzes (14th–16th C). Beyond the Sala del Palma is the *Gabinetti degli Ori*, which contains a precious collection of ancient jewellery and goldsmiths' work, medieval religious bronzes and Limoges enamels.

**Botticelli** *The Virgin and the Child* (1480)

The *Sala del Settecento Veneto* has works by **Francesco Guardi**, **Rosalba Carriera**, and **Giambattista Tiepolo**. The *Sala del Perugino* features works by **Cima da Conegliano**, Francesco Morone, Andrea Previtali, Mariotto Albertinelli (a tiny portable altar), Perugino, Biagio di Antonio di Firenze, and **Lorenzo Lotto**.

On the ground floor is the *Sala dell'Affresco*, named after its ceiling fresco by Carlo Innocenzo Carloni. A splendid Persian carpet with hunting scenes, signed and dated 1542–43, is displayed here, together with other precious carpets and tapestries, shown on a rotating basis.

A room off the entrance hall displays the *armoury*. Count Gian Giacomo Poldi Pezzoli had supported the insurgents during the *Cinque Giornate* ('five days' in 1848), when the Milanese rose up against the Austrians. As an act of reprisal, the Austrians broke into the Poldi Pezzoli armoury and Poldi was also fined heavily when Marshal Radetzky restored order for Austria. However, Poldi Pezzoli fled to Switzerland, turning his exile into a splendid European tour.

# Museo Bagatti Valsecchi

| | |
|---|---|
| **OPEN** | The museum is open 1 pm–5.45 pm, Tue-Sun, Sept-July. |
| **CLOSED** | Mon, all of August, 1/1 6/1, Easter Sunday and Whit Monday, 25/4, 1/5, 15/8, 1/11, 7-8/12, 24-31/12 |
| **CHARGES** | Regular admission €6; under 18 and over 60 €2.58. Cumulative ticket with Museo Poldi Pezzoli €7.23. |
| **GUIDED VISITS** | Audio guides available; guided visits by appointment at 02 7600 6132 |
| **DISABLED ACCESS** | Yes (ask at Reception) |
| **SERVICES** | Bookshop |
| **TELEPHONE** | 02 7600 6132 |
| **WEB** | www.bagattivalsecchi.house.museum |

**MAIN ENTRANCE**  Via Gesù 5/Via Santo Spirito 10
**GETTING THERE**  M1 to San Babila, M3 to Montenapoleone; tram 1; bus 54, 61,
65, 73 or 97

This lovely townhouse was built by the brothers Fausto and
Giuseppe Bagatti Valsecchi in 1876–87 in the style of the Lombard
Renaissance, and furnished by them richly with 16th-C works of
art and excellent 19th-C imitations by Lombard craftsmen. It was
the family home until 1974, when the Bagatti Valsecchi
established a foundation and sold the palace to the government
of Lombardy. The palace—opened to the public in 1994 as a
private museum, carefully looked after by volunteers—and the
works inside represent an interesting example of the eclectic
taste of 19th-C collectors. The house's main façade is in Via Santo
Spirito (opposite another fine palace in red brick, also built by the
brothers in 1895 in a 15th-C style).

The main staircase leads up to a vestibule, beyond which a marble
portal carved in 1884 in Renaissance style gives access to the *Sala
dell'Affresco*, with a fresco by Antonio Boselli (1496).

Beyond the panelled library, with a collection of 17th-C sundials,
is Fausto's bedroom, with an intricately carved 16th-C bed and two
paintings by Giampietrino. Beyond the dressing room and
bathroom, with ingenious plumbing masked by Renaissance
carvings, is the *Galleria della Cupola*, containing a collection of
ceramics.

The three rooms of Giuseppe's apartment have a magnificent
old stove, a late-15th-C Venetian painting of the *Blessed Lorenzo
Giustiniani*, a painting attributed to **Giovanni Bellini** and an early
17th-C Sicilian bed.

The *drawing room* is the largest room in the house, with a 19th-C
fireplace (made up of 16th-C fragments) and red wall hangings.
The long *Galleria delle Armi* was created to display the collection of
16th- and 17th-C armour, while the drawing room has a pair of
sideboards, one 16th-C and one a 19th-C copy. The walls are
covered with 16th-C tapestries and the cupboards contain 16th-C
Murano glass and Faenza ceramics.

# in the area

**Archbishops' Palace** The residence of Milan's archbishops—built by Pellegrino Tibaldi (after 1570) with a façade by Giuseppe Piermarini (1784–1801)—faces Piazza Fontana. This square witnessed with one of the more disquieting episodes in recent Italian history: in 1969 a terrorist bomb killed 16 people here (and wounded 88). **Map p. 8, 3C**

**Galleria Vittorio Emanuele II** The north side of Piazza del Duomo is connected with Piazza della Scala by the colossal Galleria Vittorio Emanuele II. This huge glass-roofed shopping arcade, with cafés and restaurants, was designed in 1865 by Giuseppe Mengoni, who fell from the top to his death a few days before the inauguration ceremony in 1878. Mengoni's design combines a severely classical style with a remarkable sensitivity for new materials such as iron. The gallery was part of a grand project to renovate Piazza del Duomo, and its success led to the construction of numerous imitations in other Italian cities, notably the Galleria Mazzini in Genoa, the Galleria Principe in Naples and the Galleria Sciarra in Rome. See p. 37 for more about the Galleria's stores. **Map p. 8, 2B**

**Museo Manzoniano** At Via Morone 1 is the house where Alessandro Manzoni (1785–1873), author of *I Promessi Sposi* ('The Betrothed'), lived from 1814 until his death. Now a museum (open Tues-Fri and Sat, 9 am–12 pm and 2 pm–4 pm, closed holidays; 02 86460), it contains mementoes of Italy's most famous novelist. *The Betrothed* is historical fiction, praised for its psychological depth and the vividness with which it portrays the Milan of the mid 17th C, including the devastating plague. The novel is now regarded as one of the most important modern Italian works. **Map p. 8, 2B**

**Museo di Milano** At Via Sant'Andrea 6 (02 7600 6245), the 18th-C Palazzo Morando houses the Museo di Milano. This interesting collection of paintings, drawings and prints depicts the changing face of Milan from the 16th C onwards. Here you can see what Milan looked like when it was criss-crossed by canals (most of which were filled in and paved over in the 20th C). Filippo Carcano's *Il Naviglio di Via Senato* (1870-75), shows a canal whose waters bordered the gardens of the houses in Via della Spiga, just a few paces from the museum. The building was Gestapo headquarters during World War II. **Map p. 8, 1B**

**Palazzo Marino** The town hall has a fine façade on Piazza San Fedele by Galeazzo Alessi (1553–58), who also designed the splendid Mannerist courtyard. The façade on Piazza Scala was completed by Luca Beltrami (1886–92). **Map p. 8, 2-3B**

**Palazzo della Ragione** This fine palace erected in 1228–33, has an upper level added in 1771 and remains of 13th-C frescoes inside. A remarkable equestrian relief of 1233 adorns its rear wall in the peaceful Piazza Mercanti. In this old square are the Gothic Loggia degli Osii (1316) and the Baroque Palazzo delle Scuole Palatine (1645). **Map p. 8, 2C**

**San Babila and its environs** From behind the duomo, Corso Vittorio Emanuele, a pedestrian street with numerous shops and arcades as well as theatres and hotels, leads through a modern area. On the left is the classic portico of the round church of San Carlo al Corso (1839–47), modelled on the Pantheon, and on the right, at the beginning of Corso Venezia, is San Babila, a 12th-C church over-restored at the end of the 19th C. At Corso Venezia 11 is the monumental gateway of the former seminary (1564), with huge caryatids; opposite is Casa Fontana, now Casa Silvestri (No. 10), with interesting terracotta work of c. 1475. There are many fine mansions of the 18th and 19th centuries, including the Neo-classical Palazzo Serbelloni (No. 16) by Simone Cantoni (1793), Palazzo Castiglioni (No. 47; 1900–04), a famous Art Nouveau palace, and Palazzo Saporiti (no. 40), built in 1812. The Corso then continues on to the Giardini Pubblici (see p. 86). **Map p. 9, 1B**

**San Pietro in Gessate** (entered from Via Chiossetto) This is a Gothic church built c. 1475. In the last chapel in the south aisle is a very damaged detached fresco of the *Funeral of St Martin* by Bergognone. The Cappella Grifo has interesting remains of frescoes depicting the life of St Ambrose (1490–93), the best-preserved part of which is the vault with delightful angels. In the south transept is an unusual painting of the *Madonna and Child* by a follower of Leonardo. Opposite San Pietro, in the Corso di Porta Vittoria, is the huge Palazzo di Giustizia (1932–40) by Marcello Piacentini. **Map p. 9, 2C**

**Santa Maria della Passione** This huge church, founded c. 1485, contains a fine series of portraits of popes and monks (in matching frames), some by Daniele Crespi. The chapels in the south aisle have Lombard frescoes and altarpieces of the 16th–17th C. In the crossing, beneath the fine dome, is another series of paintings (in their original frames) of the Passion, one by Crespi. In the south and north transepts are altarpieces by Bernardino Luini, Gaudenzio Ferrari and Giulio Campi. The chapels in the north aisle have more 16th–17th-C works, including one by Crespi.

Various rooms of the former convent and the museum can usually be visited on request. Beyond the old sacristy is the chapter house, decorated c. 1510 by Bergognone with nine paintings of Christ and the apostles opposite frescoes of saints and Doctors of the Church. Beyond is a room with a large painting, *Daniel in the Lions' Den*, by Giuseppe Vermiglio. **Map p. 9, 2C**

# commercial galleries

**Blu** Via Senato 18, 02 7602 2404, fax 02 782398, www.galleriablu.com. European modern masters: Agostino Bonalumi, Alberto Burri, Lynn Chadwick, Piero Dorazio, Max Ernst, Lucio Fontana, Pinot Gallizio, Alberto Giacometti, Vasily Kandinsky, Paul Klee, Yves Klein, Gastone Novelli, Pablo Picasso, Giuseppe Santomaso. **Map p. 9, 1A**

**Karsten Greve** Via Santo Spirito 13, 02 783840, fax 02 783866. International contemporary art, especially blue-chip. **Map p. 8, 3A**

**Guastalla** Via Senato 24, 02 780918, www.guastalla.com. European modern masters: Agostino Bonalumi, Massimo Campigli, Giuseppe Capogrossi, Giorgio De Chirico, Renato Guttoso, Emilio Isgrò, Giacomo Manzù, Marino Marini, Arturo Martini, Amedeo Modigliani, Zoran Music, Ottone Rosai, Gino Severini, Mario Sironi. **Map p. 9, 1A**

**San Carclo** Via Manzoni 46, 02 794218, fax 02 783578, www.sancarlogallery.it. Modern masters and regionally known contemporary artists: Eduardo Arroyo, Alfonso Borghi, Antoni Clavé, Corneille, Franco Fienga, Bengt Linström, A:R: Penck, Salvatore Sava, José Maria Sirvent. **Map p. 8, 3A**

**Tega** Via Senato 24, 02 7600 6473, fax 02 799707, www.clubart.it. Italian and international modern masters and blue-chip artists: Fernando Botero, Massimo Campigli, Sandro Chia, Christo, Pietro Consagra, Giorgio De Chirico, Filippo De Pisis, Lucio Fontana, Riccardo Gusmaroli, Julio Larraz, Fausto Melotti, Giorgio Morandi, Achille Perilli, Mimmo Rotella, Alberto Savinio. **Map 9, 1A**

# eat

## RESTAURANTS

€ **La Rinascente** Piazza del Duomo. This department store restaurant offers a spectacular view of the spires of the Duomo—as well as three options for lunch. For a *panino* in the main bar area, expect to pay about €5. If you want something more substantial, then a main dish at the 'Brunch' restaurant will cost €9. If you want a full meal, try the Bistrot, where three courses come in at about €30. To get there, take the escalators to the top floor. The Bistrot is closed Sundays, Mon lunchtime, and part of August. **Map p. 8, 2C**

**Boeucc** Piazza Belgioioso 2, 02 7602 0224. Elegant, sophisticated restaurant full of the movers and shakers of Milan (although you might not know their faces). Boeucc specialises in typical Milanese cuisine, thus risotto, *cotoletta alla milanese* (breaded veal), osso bucco, and more. Reservations essential. Closed Saturdays, Sun lunchtime, all of August and from Dec 24–Jan 3. **Map p. 8, 3C**

€€ **Rêve Café** Via della Spiga 42, 02 7600 1505. At a restaurant on one of the very chicest of chic streets in Milan, Masahiko Yagi and his partner Ivan Pinter experiment with fusion cuisine and make sure everything tastes as good as it looks. (That it's the only place to eat on Via della Spiga also adds to its cachet.) Rêve is open until 11 pm, which—surprising as it may sound—is late for a Milanese restaurant. Closed Sundays, and August 4–25. Reservations essential. **Map p. 9, 1B**

**La Volpe e l'Uva** Via Senato 25, 02 7602 2167. This is convenient if you are in the fashion district, especially as there is a real lack of good places in the area. This tiny restaurant is run by two sisters: Cristina does the cooking, and what she cooks is mostly tuna—fresh and delicious. Try the tuna and smoked salmon carpaccio, or a seared fillet of tuna served with lemon, oil and a touch of chilli. (Even though Milan is not on the coast, in general you can expect fresh fish. Have a look at Da Claudio at Via Ponte Vetero 16 to see an outstanding display). At lunch La Volpe e l'Uva hosts a business crowd, but in the evenings the mood changes completely, and becomes ideal for a romantic dinner. Closed Saturdays and Sundays, as well as Weds evenings and parts of August. Reservations essential. **Map 9, 1A**

**Marino alla Scala Ristorante** Piazza della Scala 5, 02 8068 8201. It's located on the first floor of Palazzo Marino alla Scala, which is immediately to your left as you look at La Scala. It specialises in creative Mediterranean cuisine. Ideal for a business lunch or an evening with friends. Closed Sundays and Sat lunchtime. Reservations essential. If you want something a little less formal but enjoy the Trussardi feel, check out the Marino alla Scala Café on the ground floor. Stone, steel, slate, and glass have been wrought into a handsome place open from 7.30 am–10 pm. Closed Sundays. Both the restaurant and the café are also closed in August and between Christmas and Jan 6. For more about the Palazzo, see www.trussardi.com. **Map p. 8, 2B**

**La Terrazza di Via Palestro** Swiss Centre, Via Palestro 2, 02 7603 3328. If it seems odd to be directed to a restaurant in the Swiss Centre when you are in Italy, just wait: it gets odder. This restaurant, with its handsome terrace overlooking the Giardini Pubblici, serves Japanese fusion Italian-style. One example is *riso bianco con caponata di melanzane e gambero*, with white rice and shrimp set off by chopped and fried eggplant served with capers, olives and celery. Probably one of the best-known Italian sauces for pasta, pesto— which is basil, garlic, and grated pecorino cheese pounded in a mortar—makes the perfect complement to white rice served with scorpion fish and toasted pine nuts. (If you prefer something more traditional, then choose from the main menu, where the style is creative Italian.) **Map p. 9, 1A**

**€€€Bice** Via Borgospesso 12, 02 7600 2572. Considering its location, between Via Montenapoloene and Via della Spiga, 'upscale' would seem to be an appropriate way to describe the restaurant called Bice (it's a nickname for Beatrice, the name of the original owner). This is one of the city's legendary restaurants, so expect traditional Milanese cuisine, such as saffron risotto or *stracotto con polenta*, and a formal atmosphere. Closed Mondays, Tues lunchtime and all of August. Reservations essential. **Map p. 8, 3A**

**Don Carlos** Via Manzoni 29, 02 7231 4640. The restaurant of the Grand Hotel et de Milan is a fashionable place to dine post-theatre, since the kitchen is one of the few that stays open until midnight. Associations with La Scala and Giuseppe Verdi (he kept an apartment here) mean that the décor is opera memorabilia. The menu, though, doesn't reflect the past: the offerings are quite creative. Try the *tagliatelle all'uovo* with sea urchins and fresh tomatoes, or the roast lamb with coffee sauce. Open only for dinner; closed Sundays. **Map p. 8, 3A**

**Mauro** Via Colonnetta 5 (on the corner of Via Cesare Battisti), 02 546 1380. It's worth a detour to get to this quiet restaurant, which specialises in traditional fish dishes and is open Sundays: remarkably unusual in Italy, where Sundays bring a meal at home or a trip to the countryside. Closed Mondays, Sat lunchtime, and all of August. Reservations essential for dinner. **Map p. 9, 1C**

## A BITE AT LUNCHTIME

**Bottiglieria da Pino** Via Cerva 14, 02 7600 0532. About halfway down the street on the right as you come from Largo Augusto, on the left from Via Borgogna, is a lunchroom behind a bar. It's packed with office workers Mon–Fri and local residents on Saturdays. There's a €13 set menu and a short list of à la carte. Service is quick and attentive, brisk without being brusque. Expect to wait for a table during the week. Closed Sundays, August and from Christmas to Jan 6. The bar itself, which is open from 8 am–8 pm, is a great place for a cappuccino and brioche or a quick glass of prosecco at aperitivo time. **Map p. 9, 1C**

## STANDBYS

**€€ Di Gennaro** Via Santa Radegonda 14, 02 8056108/02 8053454. Located right behind the Rinascente department store, this large, busy, and friendly restaurant is ideal for a pizza or for a full meal. Open every day. **Map p. 8, 3B**

**Pizzeria Dogana** Via Dogana 3, 02 805 6766. As with most pizza restaurants, you are not limited just to that. Have pasta, or a meat or fish dish, or pasta followed by a green salad. Then sweets from the trolley. This restaurant is not huge but has three discrete dining areas that give an intimate feeling. In summer, there are tables outside and it is surprisingly pleasant, since Via Dogana is pedestrianised. The ground floor is an 'eat and run' place, and the TV is often on (especially when there is a football match in progress). The downstairs is more elegant and the mood more relaxed. Closed Wednesdays. **Map p. 8, 2C**

**Prima Fila** Via Ugo Foscolo 1, 02 862020. A useful place to know of, as it is very convenient to all the shopping. Located between the Galleria Vittorio Emanuele and the Rinascente department store the restaurant has a long menu, and what they do, they do well. Lots of space, so no need to wait. Closed Wednesdays. **Map p. 8, 3C**

**Replay Piazzetta** Pattari 2, 02 86463125/02 86464106. In a little street parallel to Corso Vittorio Emanuele, less than 200 m from the

Duomo. Always busy, but you never have to wait long for a table. Lots of pizzas, but you can also choose pasta, meat, or fish. Closed Sundays. **Map p. 8, 3C**

**€€€Nabucco** Via Fiori Chiari 10, 02 860663. Not only is this restaurant in the very heart of the Brera district open daily, but the kitchen closes at 11.30 pm, which is a rarity in Milan. Home-made pasta and fresh fish, along with local Milanese specialities. **Map p. 8, 2A**

# WINE BARS

**€€ Taverna Visconti** Via Marziale 11, 02 795 821. This wine bar is in a quiet side street just off Piazza San Babila. The building is an early 19th-C patrician home, the sort Stendhal might have visited during his stay in Milan. There are a mere six tables in the bistrot, but if you get a seat you can choose from the blackboard and order wine by the glass or the bottle. For a more leisurely evening, try the restaurant in the cellar. The cuisine is traditional: shrimp with spinach-flavoured polenta, steak with balsamic vinegar, and *cotoletta alla milanese*. Closed Sundays, Sat lunchtime and all of August. **Map p. 9, 1C**

# CAFÉS

**€ Camparino** Piazza del Duomo, corner of Galleria Vittorio Emanuele. This is probably the best-known of the cafés in the Galleria Vittorio Emanuele. Davide Campari, inventor of Campari, was born here on the first floor, where his parents—who ran the bar—lived. The décor is early 20th-C: the bar and the mosaics were designed by Eugenio Quarti, while the chandelier is the work of Alessandro Mazzucotelli. But even better than sitting inside and admiring the mosaics is sitting outside, sip a pre-lunch or pre-dinner aperitivo and watch the people go by. Open Thur–Tues, 7.30 am–8.30 pm. **Map p. 8, 2C**

**€€ Biffi** Galleria Vittorio Emanuele II. Biffi is also one of the ever-decreasing number of cafés in the Galleria (Il Salotto now having become another Gucci store) and, although much altered over the years, a very famous name. It's not to be confused with the store called Biffi in Corso Genova; Biffi is a just a Milanese family name (as is Prada). **Map p. 8, 2B**

# shop

There's a wealth of shopping in the city centre, but unless you are looking for a specific boutique, you'll have the most fun if you just follow your feet, follow your eyes and—more than anything—follow everyone else. (To find a particular shop, see our lists below, which are divided by neighbourhood.)

## MONTENAPOLEONE

The area around Via Montenapoleone (**Maps p. 8, 3A-B, and p. 9, 1A-B**) is Milan's famous fashion district. The great designers have their showrooms on Via Sant'Andrea, Via della Spiga, Via Gesù, Via Borgospesso, Via Santo Spirito, Via Verri and, of course, Via Montenapoleone. The so-called *Triangolo della Moda* area has expanded in recent times to include Via Manzoni, from the Piazza Cavour end, and Corso Venezia, from Piazza San Babila to Via Senato.

Since it's almost a rite of passage for a designer at least to open a shop in this area, if not to succeed there, the names above the doors change regularly. We've tried to stick to the tried and true, along with some of the more interesting newcomers.

Store hours in this area are from about 10.30 am–7.30 pm, Mon–Sat. Stores are open Sundays in the run-up to Christmas and also on the da;y of the Milan Furniture Fair in April. Listings are alphabetical order by street, and streets have been listed in the order you might actually meander, but turning down a lane to catch a glimpse of some intriguing shop window is part of the experience, so don't be afraid to stray.

## VIA MANZONI

**Map p. 8, 3A**

**Armani** Via Manzoni 31. Armani's megastore: men's and women's diffusion collections from Emporio Armani and Armani Jeans; the Armani Casa household collection; plus a florist, a bookstore, the Armani Caffè (offering, among other things, Armani pralines or assorted Armani chocolates) and the Nobu sushi restaurant.

**Patrizia Pepe** Via Manzoni 38. Originally a company that manufactured apparel for third parties, Patrizia Pepe has been out on her own for about five years. Chic separates at prices you would not expect in this prime location.

**Strenesse** Via Manzoni 37. If you like Armani you might look at Gabriele Strehle's creations for Strenesse; the Milan store of this German maker of upscale womenswear (and recently, menswear) plays to the same crowd.

**Ventilo** Via Manzoni 25. See what this French store offers in the way of ethnic-inspired clothing, as well as more understated lines. There's a home collection upstairs.

## MAKING A FASHION STATEMENT
**Trussardi Palazzo Marino alla Scala** Piazza della Scala 5 (02 8068 8242). Men's and women's leather goods and accessories are on the ground floor, and there is café and a restaurant upstairs (see p. 28). If you remember the exhibition space and bookstore, there are no more. The Fondazione Nicola Trussardi is still sponsoring contemporary art, though. If you are in town in May and November, look for their eye-catching site-specific installations (www.fondazionenicolatrussardi.com). For the menswear and womenswear, head for Via Sant'Andrea 5. For the Trussardi Jeans and Sportswear collections, check out T'store in Via Durini on the corner of the Galleria Strasburgo. www.trussardi.com.

# VIA MONTENAPOLEONE
**Maps p. 8, 3B, and p. 9, 1B**

**Alberta Ferretti** Via Montenapoleone 19–21. Alberta Ferretti in one store and Alberta Ferretti Philosophy, designed for a younger audience, in the other.

**Armani Collezioni** Via Montenapoleone 2. This is where what the Italians call 'the first line' of Armani is sold, and it's sold with the atmosphere to match. Here at the top, service is key. See also the Armani superstore at Via Manzoni 31 (p. 31).

**Céline** Via Montenapoleone 25. A chic look for a French company that also does an attractive line in handbags.

**Christian Dior** Via Montenapoleone 12–14. Vast plate-glass windows allow you to see inside, and fans of the Dior look will find their feet inevitably straying towards the entrance.

**Emanuel Ungaro** Via Montenapoleone 27. Part of the Ferragamo stable, this French fashion house—which recently quit the 'haute couture' field to stick with ready-made—offers a more sober answer to the eternal question of 'what to wear?'.

**Emilio Pucci** Via Montenapoleone 14. This is one of the oldest and best-known brands in Italian fashion.

**Etro** Via Montenapoleone 5. Paisley patterns (in Italian called *cachemere*, not to be confused with the fabric of the same name) are Etro's distinguishing feature. Not that the clothes, bags, accessories, leather goods, and household goods are covered in them, of course. See also the perfumes of the line at Etro Profumi, the corner of Via Verri and Via Bigli.

**Gianni Versace** Via Montenapoleone 11. Menswear and womenswear, also skincare and cosmetics. Head for the Versus store at Via San Pietro all'Orto 10 for Versace Jeans and Sport, as well as the children's lines. Cross the street for the Versace Home Collection.

**Gucci** Via Montenapoleone 5/7. Everything Gucci, and Gucci style needs no introduction to the world of fashion.

**Iceberg** Via Montenapoleone 10. The ideal label for those looking for a cool look, but one that does not necessarily scream 'fashion!' as loudly as it can. There is also a fragrance line.

**Loro Piana** Via Montenapoleone 27c. The ultimate in cashmere softness; ready-to-wear for men and women as well as homewear and sumptuous accessories; top-notch made-to-measure suits with prices to match.

**Mariella Burani** Via Montenapoleone 3. The boutique, a haven for the romantic, the dressy and the classic, has been here since 1985, which makes it positively ancient in terms of longevity for designer boutiques in the *Triangolo*. The turnover is extraordinary. For many of the items in the collection, it's a case of 'Now you see them, now you don't', so if there's anything that looks good, don't pass up the opportunity.

**Miss Sixty** Via Montenapoleone 27. Small but jam-packed—with embroidered, sprayed and studded denim jeans and jackets, plus girly stuff like bags, belts and sunglasses. Also at Via Solferino 9.

**Narciso Rodriguez** Via Montenapoleone 21. An exquisitely designed boutique for this cosmopolitan designer.

**Ralph Lauren**, Via Montenapoleone 4, corner of Via Baguttino. Apparently the fruit of a ten-year search for an ideal property, the Ralph Lauren boutique opened in September 2004. All four floors are retail in what was once the home of Italian poet Carlo Porta (1775–1821).

**Yves Saint Laurent Rive Gauche** Via Montenapoleone 4. The amount of sales space on two floors makes this YSL's largest store in Europe. Menswear and womenswear, footwear, handbags, right through to cosmetics.

## VIA DELLA SPIGA
### Map p. 9, 1A-B

**Agnona** Via della Spiga 3. The womenswear of Ermenegildo Zegna. Everything cashmere, from apparel to scarves, with extras such as cashmere teddy bears and slippers.

**Dolce&Gabbana** Via della Spiga 26. Inaugurated in the autumn of 2004, this 900-m3 boutique is womenswear all the way. Black, the dominant colour, sets off the Neo-Baroque furniture, Murano glass light fixtures, magnificent cactuses, metals, mirrors and video screens. For women's accessories, walk down to Via della Spiga 2, by the corner of Corso Venezia, and turn right to reach No. 15 for menswear. No. 7 houses the diffusion collections, including swimwear, underwear, accessories, timepieces and eyewear.

**Fay** Via della Spiga 15. Launched by a fire-fighter's jacket with its signature four metal hooks in the 1980s, Diego della Valle's Fay brand has grown over the years. The Fay flagship store, inaugurated in November 2002, was designed by Philip Johnson, and could almost be mistaken for an elegant living room: light ochre and ivory paintwork, with olivewood furniture and natural stone floors.

**Gio Moretti** Via della Spiga 4. The selection is hand-picked by store owner Gio Moretti herself, and includes the best of Roberto Cavalli, Chloé, DKNY, Jean Paul Gaultier, Ralph Lauren, Plein Sud, Jil Sander and many other labels under one roof. Also a home collection, books and CDs.

**Malo** Via della Spiga 7. Colourful, soft, luxurious cashmere sweaters, scarves and gloves, as well as an expanding ready-to-wear collection. Also cushions, throws, and other accessories for the home.

**Moschino** Via della Spiga 30. On street level, the Chic and Cheap collection. Descend the red stairway to explore the jeans and menswear, as well as the children's and juniors' department. Also Via Sant'Andrea 12, where the highly innovative window displays are a major feature of the streetscape.

**Roberto Cavalli** Via della Spiga 42. Two floors and three huge display windows on the street, for those for whom hyper-glamorous is a positive term. Everything from underwear to shoes to a home collection. Fans of the leopard-skin look may like to check out the Just Cavalli café.

# VIA VERRI
## Map p. 8, 3B

**Alexander McQueen** Via Verri 8. See this British designer's latest ideas in a street with some very browseable menswear stores.

**Ermenegildo Zegna** Via Verri 3. Italy's finest made-to-measure and ready-to-wear menswear is tucked away in a quiet corner away from the hustle and bustle. If you are female, head for Agnona, at Via della Spiga (see p. 34), where you can find Zegna's take on womenswear: cashmere all the way.

**Etro** Corner of Via Verri and Via Bigli. Pretty little store full of fragrances to sample and buy. The company has a boutique at Via Montenapoleone 5 (see p. 33).

**Jil Sander** Via Verri 6. Never one for overstatement, German designer Jil Sander offers quietly chic collections for the classically minded.

**John Richmond** Corner of Via Verri and Via Bigli. British designer John Richmond's rock'n'roll rebel style; a selection of CDs and magazines adds to the vibe.

## VIA SANT'ANDREA
**Map p. 9, 1B**

**Giorgio Armani** Via Sant'Andrea 9. The venerable house.

**Antonio Fusco** Via Sant'Andrea 11. Sleek, clean-cut lines form the style for this boutique, reflecting the Antonio Fusco look of perfectly tailored yet easy-to-wear elegance. Menswear and womenswear.

**Banner** Via Sant'Andrea 8. Designed by Gae Aulenti, Milanese architect and designer of the renovated Musée d'Orsay museum in Paris, Banner is one-stop shopping for those in search of sophisticated chic: Emilio Pucci, John Galliano, Yohji Yamamoto, Junya Watanabe, Alberto Biani, Dries van Noten and Viktor&Rolf.

**Chanel** Via Sant'Andrea 10a, close to the corner of Via della Spiga.

**Costume National** Via Sant'Andrea 12. Despite the French name, as Italian as they come. Check out the eye-catching boutique, as well as the clothing: high-tech fabrics and a basic colour palette dominated by black, white and pale pastels; also shoes, belts, bags, leather accessories, fragrances.

**Fendi** Via Sant'Andrea 16. On the ground floor, handbags, luggage, timepieces and womenswear. First floor is all furs.

**Gianfranco Ferré** Via Sant'Andrea 15. Since the Corso Venezia store closed, this is the only GFF store in town. While you are here, check out the spa, with facials, steam and mud treatments (02 7601 7526). Reservations essential, preferably one week in advance. If your appointment is after the store closes, ring the bell.

**Moschino** Via Sant'Andrea 12. Moschino womenswear in this beautifully designed store, created with the assistance of architect Sean Dix. The Moschino genius for extraordinarily exciting window displays lives on.

**Trussardi** Via Sant'Andrea 5. Trussardi have been in this location for years—now the space has menswear and womenswear. For the Trussardi Jeans and Sportswear collections, check out T'store in Via Durini on the corner of the Galleria Strasburgo. Do not miss Trussardi's flagship building at Palazzo Marino alla Scala, either (see p. 32).

## OFF THE MAP

**Marni** Via Sant'Andrea 14. Bohemian romance from an Italian designer who's probably best known in the UK. If you are here for a few days, take the 61 bus to the terminus at Largo Murani and visit the Marni outlet in Via Tajani. Open early Oct–early July.

# GALLERIA VITTORIO EMANUELE

Fast coming up as a competitor to via Montenapoleone is the Galleria Vittorio Emanuele (**Map p. 8, 2B**). Previously only Prada had a store there—they've been tenants since the early 1900s, when Fratelli Prada were producers of luggage for people who took their travel seriously. In the summer of 2004, Louis Vuitton took over a huge spot right at the centre of the Galleria, while Gucci snapped up a bar—La Saletta—and made it into a store.

**Gucci** Opened in September 2004, this space used to be a café and now offers 180 m2 of Gucci accessories on two floors. The world's first Gucci bar is due to open as the book goes to press. For apparel, head for Gucci in Via Montenapoleone 5/7 (see p. 33).

**Louis Vuitton** Opened in September 2004, Vuitton's new flagship store takes up one segment of the octagonal space in the very centre of the Galleria. Travel cases, briefcases, belts, scarves—countless Louis Vuitton accessories are here under one roof.

**Luisa Spagnoli** This Perugia-based family company started out manufacturing exquisite cashmere knits, and then—in the late-1960s—became Italy's first chain boutique. Eye-catching colours, unusual styles, pleasant sales staff, and competitive prices in the upper-middle range.

**Prada** This is a store worth seeing. The black-and-white floor, exquisite shop fittings commissioned from a London firm in 1913, and murals on the lower floor are gorgeous, but don't overshadow the apparel, or the bags—which is where the whole story started, in the early days of the 20th C, Mario Prada, grandfather of current Prada head Miuccia Prada, started Prada as a maker of leather bags, trunks and travel accessories. The look of the flagship store here in the Galleria has remained the same partly because of unfortunate circumstances: the Galleria was bombed in 1943 but Prada didn't have enough money to completely redecorate the store and had to make do with salvaged remainders. For more about the Prada Foundation, see p. 42. There are also Prada stores at Via Montenapoleone 6 (menswear), Via Montenapoleone 8 (womens

**Galleria Vittorio Emanuele II**

wear), Via della Spiga 1 (accessories), Via della Spiga 5 (lingerie), Via Sant'Andrea 21 (sportswear), and Corso Venezia (Miu Miu).

**Tod's** Located in the section of the Galleria that leads towards Via Silvio Pellico and on to Cordusio, this elegant boutique opened in September 2004 and features womenswear, menswear and children's wear, along with bags, and accessories.

## CORSO VITTORIO EMANUELE TO PIAZZA SAN BABILA
Maps p. 8, 3C, and p. 9, 1B

Corso Vittorio Emanuele, which links the Duomo to Piazza San Babila, is, in some ways, Milan's high street. Here's where you can find the international chains, such as Benetton, Sisley, Zara and the like. Now a pedestrian precinct, it is popular with residents as well as visitors. If you want to watch the world go by, then take a seat at one of the sidewalk cafés (they have heaters in the winter).

**Benetton** Corso Vittorio Emanele 9. Also Corso Buenos Aires, and Corso Vercelli. Another of the ubiquitous stores.

**Fiorucci Love Therapy** Corso Europa, corner of Galleria Passarella. If you were wondering what happened to the old Fiorucci store, at the bottom of Corso Vittorio Emanuele on the curve just before you get to Piazza San Babila, it became H&M in the summer of 2003 when Elio Fiorucci declared he had had enough of retail, and was going to do something else. So now, one year on, he has opened another store, full of his signature bright colours on T-shirts, jeans, candles, key rings, and other similar items.

**Guess?** Piazza San Babila 4b. The LA womenswear label offers everything from jeans to backless evening dresses, with strappy shoes and sandals to match.

**Hugo Boss** Via Matteotti 11. Everything Boss, for men and women, in the company's Italy flagship store.

**JDC Urban Store** Piazza Duomo 31. JDC's own collection of denims, along with labels such as Guru, Levi's, Lonsdale, Diesel, Industrie, Woolrich and Puma attract a young, fashion-conscious crowd. If you enjoy shopping in total darkness, this is the place for you. Also at Corso Buenos Aires 56, corner of Via Ponchielli.

**Marina Rinaldi** Corso Vittorio Emanuele, corner of Galleria Passarella. Part of the Max Mara empire, the Marina Rinaldi collection for full-figured women is a classic look: suits, knits and tailored basics, eveningwear and sportswear, as well as shoes and handbags.

**Nadine** Corso Vittorio Emanuele 63, corner of Galleria Passarella. Style-savvy stuff at mid-range prices for a young crowd. Also at Via Dante 16 and Corso Buenos Aires 38.

**Onyx Fashion Store** Corso Vittorio Emanuele 24. You have to go up the escalator to reach the store, a strange effect, and it's best visited with a teenager. Lots of backpacks and other school accessories. Also at Via Torino 2.

**Max Mara** Corso Vittorio Emanuele, corner Galleria de Cristoforis. Max Mara's famous camel-hair coats, accompanied by the whole family of Max Mara brands—Sportmax, Weekend and Max Mara Basic—and by a wide range of accessories, from shoes to handbags to silk scarves. Also at Via Cuneo 3, Via Victor Hugo 1, corner of Via Orefici. Also check out Diffusione Tessile.

**Max & Co** Corso Vittorio Emanuele. Right next to the designer's main store is MaxMara's younger, trendier label, with clever women's clothing and a good range of shoes, handbags and bags and scarves. Also at Via Dante 7 (Duomo), and Corso Vercelli 11. Also check out Diffusione Tessile.

**Replay** Corso Vittorio Emanuele, corner Largo Corsia dei Servi. If nothing else, check out the store for the imaginative desplay designs. Every section is different. Jeans and casual fashions; also a colourful children's collection.

**Sisley** Piazza del Duomo, at the Via Mazzini corner. The more upscale Benetton brand. Also at Corso Vercelli 9. There's no connection with the cosmetics company, by the way.

**Stefanel** Corso Vittorio Emanuele 28. Colourful separates; middle-market prices. Also Via Spadari 1.

**Zap!** Galleria Passarella 2. Innovative retail design for Milan, this giant multibrand store on three floors features, among others, Anna Sui, Gaetano Navarro, Holly, Kookaï, Liu-Jo, Santa Croce, plus books, accessories and even collectors' edition Barbies. Also, children's and vintage clothes, magazines and books, as well as state-of-the-art consumer electronics.

**Zara** Galleria Vittorio Emanuele 11. Zara is worth looking at for the store design alone. The company spent years seeking the right location and—when this 1930s cinema closed down, they moved in. The atrium sports a beautiful chandelier, while the curved staircase adds grace to a delightful setting. The clothes are worth looking at, to compare with what Barcelona-based Zara offers in London and elsewhere; see if it is true here, as it has been with other labels, that quality had to improve to make headway in Italy, where shoppers are more demanding. Also in Corso Buenos Aires.

# CORSO VENEZIA
## Maps p. 8, 3C, and p. 9, 2B

**Borsalino** Corso Venezia corner of Via Senato. Complementing the tiny store in the Galleria Vittorio Emanuele at the Piazza della Scala end, this store (opened in September 2004) has generous floor space and seven display windows. Admire the hats, for both men and women, and take a look at the brass and crystal columns and the lighting fixtures, which are by Artemide.

**D&G** Corso Venezia 7. Dolce&Gabbana diffusion, includes swimwear, underwear, accessories, timepieces, and eyewear. For menswear, check out No. 15. For women's accessories, go to Via della Spiga 2, which is on the corner, just a little further along Corso Venezia. Keep going in Via della Spiga, across Via Sant'Andrea until you get to No. 26 to find the womenswear boutique.

**Dolce&Gabbana**, Corso Venezia 15. Inaugurated in April 2004, this early 19th-C patrician home is now Dolce&Gabbana's menswear boutique with some 1,700 m2 on three floors. Men can check out the barber (02 7640 8881), women can stop by the beautician's or call 02 76408888 for an appointment. If it all too much hard work, retire to the Martini Bar (02 7601 1154), open 10 am–9.30 pm, Mon–Sat. Closed Sundays.

**Miu Miu** Corso Venezia 3. Miu Miu is Miuccia Prada, whose last name is synonymous with the Milan fashion phenomenon. What you see here started as her experimental collection of men's and women's apparel in 1992, when the family leather goods firm shifted its attention to the fashion arena.

# OTHER STORES

Italy is famous for its footwear and tailored menswear, and there's a great deal of both in the city centre.

## MENSWEAR

**Brioni-Roman Style** Via Gesù 2a. Men's suits magnificently cut from the best English and Italian fabrics. Bespoke tailoring on the first floor **Map p. 9, 1A**

**Canziani** Via Montenapoleone 26. Men's ready-to-wear and made-to-measure shirts, with ties to match; also underclothes and traditional pyjamas. **Map p. 8, 3A**

**Corneliani** Via Montenapoleone 12. High-quality menswear: classic suits, shirts and ties, both ready-to-wear and made-to-measure, plus more casual clothes (such as leather jackets) from the Trend Corneliani line. **Map p. 9, 1B**

**Davide Cenci** Via Manzoni 7. Attentive service is the big selling point at this multi-brand men's and women's store: the looks tend towards the classic, and the selection is slightly more male-oriented. **Map p. 8, 3B**

**Domo Adami** Via Manzoni 23. Unusual wedding dresses designed by Mauro Adami, who favours pale colours and fitted gowns rather than fluffy, draped cuts; the firm can also help with accessories, makeup, hair and a wedding album. **Map p. 8, 3B**

**Ermenegildo Zegna** Via Verri 3. Italy's finest made-to-measure and ready-to-wear menswear tucked away in a quiet corner away from the hustle and bustle: suits, shirts, knitwear, shoes, ties, and other accessories. Agnona in Via dalla Spiga is Zegna for women. **Map p. 8, 3B**

**Gianni Campagna** Corso Venezia 53a, Via Palestro 24. In a majestic 19th-C building at the corner of Corso Venezia and Via Palestro, Gianni Campagna offers personalised precision tailoring in the finest fabrics; a more affordable ready-to-wear collection is also available, as is womenswear produced under the Baratta label. **Map p. 9, 2B**

**Larusmiani** Via Verri 10. A good source for men's sportswear and casualwear, with a varied colour scheme and a broad range of accessories. **Map p. 8, 3B**

**Umberto Bilancioni**, Via Santo Spirito 7. This eye-catching menswear store is located right by the Museo Bagatti Valsecchi (p. 22). Take the time to do both. **Map p. 8, 3B**

## FOOTWEAR

**A. Testoni** Via Montenapoleone 19. Classic, hand-crafted shoes for men and women, along with a women's collection and a range of leather bags, briefcases and belts. **Map p. 9, 1B**

**Alberto Guardiani** Via Montenapoleone 9. Shoes for the young and style-savvy, from colourful pointy mules to basic leather lace-ups, to two-tone sneaker-shoe hybrids. **Map 9, 1B**

**Baldinini** Via Montenapoleone 15. Men's and women's shoes with a marked sense of design, accompanied by matching handbags, briefcases and other leather accessories. **Map 9, 1B**

### THE PRADA FOUNDATION
As well as becoming a key player in the fashion field, Prada has made a considerable contribution to Italy's art scene. The Fondazione Prada is at Via Fogazzaro 36, on the corner of Via Cadore (02 5467 0515; www.fondazioneprada.org). Located in a former bank archive, this gallery is a spectacle in itself. There are two exhibitions a year: March to May and October to December. Previous artists have included Thomas Friedman, Michael Heizer, Anish Kapoor, Marc Quinn, and Carsten Höller. In conjunction with Fondazione Prada, in 1996 Dan Flavin created a fluorescent-light installation specifically for the Chiesa Rossa at Via Neera 24 (02 5467 0216; www.fondazione prada.org). Take tram 3 or 15. Open 4-7pm daily. Admission free.

**Shots from the Prada fall/winter 2004 collection**

shop!

**Bally** Via Montenapoleone 8. Switzerland's finest ultra-chic luxury brand: footwear, luggage, handbags and ready-to-wear. **Map p. 9, 1B**

**Bruno Magli** Corner of Corso Vittorio Emanuele and Via San Paolo, also Via Manzoni 14. Finely crafted men's shoes, an extensive collection of women's shoes, leather clothing and accessories, plus the Magli Sport line of sneakers and casual suede and leather shoes. **Map p. 8, 3C**

**Camper** Via Montenapoleone 6. Fun, unconventional shoes for men and women. **Map p. 8, 3B**

**Casadei** Via Sant'Andrea 17. These flamboyant designs score high marks with fashion followers. There is only a small men's collection. **Map p. 9, 1B**

**Cesare Paciotti** Via Sant'Andrea 8. Two floors of extravagant footwear. For women, there's black sneakers studded with Swarovski crystal and knee-high stiletto boots; for men, it's wingtips, brogues, snakeskin shoes and combat boots. **Map p. 9, 1B**

**Church's** Via Sant'Andrea 11. Acquired by Prada some years ago, this British shoemaker has probably become better known in the UK than it ever was before in its 150-year history. **Map p. 9, 1B**

**Fausto Santini** Via Montenapoleone 1. Singular designs for men and women by Rome's most brilliant shoe and handbag maker; prices are relatively reasonable given the quality and the neighbourhood. **Map p. 9, 1B**

**Frattelli Rossetti** Via Montenapoleone 1. Always one for innovation, Rossetti's men's and women's footwear is diverse, the details rich and the technique and materials perfect. **Map p. 9, 1B**

**Gastone Lucioli** Via Montenapoleone 15. Designer women's shoes with an appreciation for detail and the occasional extravagant touch: mules, pumps, sandals, and boots in leather, suede, denim and mohair. **Map p. 9, 1B**

**Hogan** Via Montenapoleone 23. The sober elegance of Diego Della Valle's Hogan footwear and accessories for men, women and children exhibit the same high quality that has given big brother label Tod's such solid standing over the years. **Map p. 8, 3B**

**René Caovilla** Via Bagutta. Not many people notice that there is a little street running parallel to Via Montenapoleone from Piazza San Babila to Via Sant'Andrea, but those that do know it mainly for the restaurants. Caovilla was one of the first fashion stores to open here (in 2004) and will probably not be the last. **Map p. 9, 1B**

**Salvatore Ferragamo** Via Montenapoleone 3 (women), Via Montenapoleone 20 (men). Worth a visit even if you're not looking for shoes, as the venerable maker of stylish leather goods and accessories is constantly expanding its lines. The women's location also has ties and a selection of gift items for men. **Map p. 9, 1B**

**Sergio Rossi** Via della Spiga 15 and Via Montenapoleone 6a. Seriously sexy shoes (for men and women) from one of Italy's leading designers; also bags and leather goods. **Map p. 9, 1A and p. 9, 1B**

**Tanino Crisci** Via Montenapoleone 3. This firm's reputation is built on riding boots (as the horse logo suggests) but there are also plenty of shoes to choose from, as well as a full range of scarves, ties, belts, bags and briefcases. **Map p. 9, 1B**

**Tod's** Via della Spiga 22. Hand-stitched leather is the stylish staple of designer Diego Della Valle's high-quality line of footwear and accessories for men, women and children; in recent years the beautiful leather bags have become as much of a draw as the shoes. **Map p. 9, 1A**

**Valeriano** Via Montenapoleone 6. Fine, handcrafted footwear: traditional loafers and lace-ups for men, more playful styles for women. **Map p. 9, 11B**

**Vergelio** Corso Vittorio Emanuele 10. Luxury shoe seller offering a wide choice of designer brands at a handful of locations around the city. **Map p. 8, 2B**

**Vicini** Via della Spiga 1. Shoes from the 1930s–1950s, updated with a modern twist. Also, eyewear, bags and belts. **Map p. 9, 1B**

**Vierre** Via Montenapoleone 29. Everything from impossibly high heels to comfortable walking shoes, by a wide range of designers: Giorgio Armani, Antonio Berardi, Gianni Barbate, René Caovilla, Roberto Cavalli, Costume National, D-Squared, Miu Miu, Michel Perry, Jil Sander and Alain Tondowski. **Map p. 9, 1B**

## JUST FOR FUN

**Ars Rosa** Via Montenapoleone 8. Everything for one's *corredo* (trousseau), including luxurious custom-made lingerie and bathrobes in silk and cashmere, embellished with embroidery and handmade lace. Also christening gowns and other special occasion babywear, plus beautiful household linen. **Map p. 9, 1B**

**Atelier Aimée** Via Montenapoleone 27e. Bridal boutique offering 300 new wedding gown designs each year, as well as chic wedding party attire. **Map p. 8, 3B**

**Barbara Bui** Via Manzoni 45. Franco-Vietnamese designer Barbara Bui is known for her precisely-tailored urban style: sleek trousers and close-cut leather blazers, tailored shirts and simple knits in classic colours—pointy stilettos and leather sneaker-shoes complete the sleek city look. www.barbarabui.com. **Map p. 8, 3A**

**Bonpoint** Via Manzoni 15. Lovely, carefully thought-out apparel for girls (up to age 16) and boys (up to age 12); the smallest things are the best. **Map p. 8, 3B**

**Cesare Gatti** Via Montenapoleone 19. If you can't find it, it's because it's in a courtyard between Testoni and Alberta Ferretti. Cashmere classics: sweaters, scarves, coats, capes, blankets. **Map p. 9, 1B**

## OUTLETS

**DMagazine Outlet** Via Montenapoleone 26. A bargain-hunter's dream, offering all sorts of previous season's collections at a discount: Armani, Cavalli, Costume National, Dsquared, Romeo Gigli, Gucci, Miu Miu, Plein Sud, Prada, Jil Sander and many more. **Map p. 8, 3A**

**Diffusione Tessile** Galleria San Carlo 6. Last season's collections from the MaxMara group at a discount, including Max Mara, Max & Co, Sportmax, Marella, Penny Black and Marina Rinaldi. Also shoes and accessories. **Map p. 9, 1B**

## DEPARTMENT STORES

There are only two nationwide chains in Italy. The more traditional—and expensive—is La Rinascente, which has about 20 outlets. COIN, which is more stylish and has quite competitive prices, has some 350. The only reason to visit a department store is to get a feel of what is on offer this season without being pestered by sales staff, and without being overwhelmed by loud music and other stylishly sense-assaulting details.

**La Rinascente** Via Santa Radegonda 3. This is the company's flagship store, with makeup, bags and eyewear on the ground floor. You can find a better clothes selection elsewhere, but the lingerie selection is extensive, with racks and racks of everything from petticoats to nightgowns. On the top floor is the Estée Lauder Spa and a café with a view of the Duomo's spires and gargoyles (see p. 27). Head for the basement for the household goods. **Map p. 8, 3B**

**COIN** Piazza Cinque Giornate. COIN department stores tend to be carved out of existing buildings (which is why you don't notice them), but the Cinque Giornate store is a highly visible eight storeys. As with the Rinascente, the ground floor is probably the most interesting, with handbags, cosmetics and accessories. The bags are particularly attractive and are very well-priced. So is the costume jewellery. The top floor of the building is a restaurant and bars, but without much of a view. COIN is also in Piazza Cantore and Corso Vercelli. **Map p. 9, 3C**

**UPIM** Piazza San Babila 5. As you may have noticed from previous visits, the UPIM department store chain has gone upmarket in recent years. Always good value, the household goods department also offers some surprisingly eye-catching items. **Map p. 9, 1B**

## WORTH MAKING A DETOUR

**10 Corso Como** The address is Corso Como 10, of course. You are probably not going to buy anything from Carla Sozzani's wildly eclectic store carved out of a typical 19th-C residential building. However, you can't say you have been to Milan if you have not paid a visit. Designers include all the cutting-edge names—some so cutting-edge you won't have heard of them. It's that kind of place. Admire the jewellery, crave the household accessories, wander round the bookshop and see one of the finest displays of art, architecture, and design publications in town, step into the record store, see the photography exhibition in the art gallery, then have a coffee in the courtyard café. Consider staying at one of the Three Rooms, 10 Corso Como's recently-opened B&B. The complex is open Monday mornings, then 3.30 pm–7.30 pm on Monday; 10.30 am–7.30 pm on Tuesday; 10.30 am–9 pm Wed–Thur, Fri–Sun. Closed during Milan Fashion week and Milan Furniture Fair and one week in August.

For the budget-minded, try the **10 Corso Como outlet** around the corner at Via Tazzoli 3. Open 1 pm–7 pm, Wed–Fri; 11 am–7 pm, Sat–Sun; closed Mon and Tues.

## BOOKS

If you are not one of the 63 million or so people in the world who speak Italian, Italian bookshops are unlikely to have much appeal. If you do speak Italian and want to stock up while you are here, you are also likely to be a little disappointed, as a good 50% of all books published in Italy are translated (for the most part from English, and often indifferently).

If the words are lacking, though, the pictures are not. Italy is famous for premier-quality colour printing, and coffee table art books printed here can be outstanding. Check them out at at the Armani superstore at Via Manzoni 31 or go to 10 Corso Como (see above). For antique books, try the American Bookstore at Via Camperio 16, which is at the top of Via

Dante and opposite the Castello Sforzesco (see p. 63). Alternatively, try and make your visit coincide with the five-day Milan Antiquarian book Fair, held in late-March each year (www.mostralibroantico.com). To go directly to the sources, try Franco Maria Ricci Editore at Via Durini 19, the flagship store of the country's premier luxury art book publisher. Open 9.30 am–1 pm and 3 pm–7.30 pm every day, but closed Mon morning.

## FOOD SHOPS

If you're in the shopping district, try Milan's spectacular deli **Il Salumaio** on Via Montenapoleone, in the courtyard of No. 12 ( **Map p. 9, 1B**). It's also a good place for lunch in this otherwise restaurant-starved zone.

And if you're by the Duomo, it's just a few steps away to the magnificent **Peck** (see p. 145).

## THE HOME

**Cassina** Via Durini 16. If you know about Italian design, you know about Cassina. Even if you are too intimidated to walk in and look around, the window display is a handsome showcase of some legendary names like Gio Ponti, Vico Magistretti and Philippe Starck. If you are interested in buying a design classic, check out the company's Great Masters initiative. Names include Gerrit Rietveld, Charles Rennie Mackintosh and Frank Lloyd Wright. **Map p. 9, 1C**

**Corso Europa Emporio Casa** Corso Europa 12. Nearly 500 m3 of cool furniture for home and office (by B&B Italia, Boffi, Cassina, Dada, Flou, Frau, Giorgetti, Knoll, Minotti, Molteni, Porro, Zanotta and more), plus a made-to-order department. **Map p. 9, 1C**

**Versace Home Collection** Via San Pietro all'Orto 10. A 'lifestyle' shop by the cutting-edge designer of luxury goods, fragrances and accessories for men and women. **Map p. 9, 1B**

**La Rinascente** Italy's premier department store (see p. 46), has an especially good housewares section, featuring Alessi and other designer names. Go to the sixth floor for household linens. Before you buy, remember that sheets in Italy are always 100% cotton, so ironing is essential to maintain that pristine look. **Map p. 8, 3B**

**Frette** Via Montenapoleone 21 and Via Manzoni 11. The ultimate place to shop for luxury linens and homewear—and for men and women's pyjamas, robes, and the like. **Map p. 9, 1B, and p. 8, 3B**

**Zucchi** Via Ugo Foscolo 4. Zucchi (and Bassetti, its mid-range subsidiary) is the best-known name in mid-priced household linens in Italy. This store lies between the Galleria and the Rinascente department store; step downstairs to see the so-called Zucchi collection. Testifying to almost two centuries of European textile production, it consists of over 56,000 blocks representing 12,000 patterns for the hand printing of materials, the first examples dating from 1785. **Map p. 8, 3B**

## JEWELLERY
**Federico Buccellati** Via della Spiga 2. One of the traditional names: the best stones and finest workmanship. **Map p. 9, 1B**

**Bulgari Italia** Via della Spiga 6. The company's original line of business. See also the fabulous assortment of accessories, such as timepieces, leather, scarves, fragrance and eyewear. **Map p. 9, 1B**

**Cusi Gioielliere** Via Montenapoleone 21a. Longstanding tradition, attention to detail and creative styling. **Map p. 8, 3B**

**Tiffany** Via della Spiga 19a. 'Simply spectacular' is the company's motto: nothing less than the finest jewellery, silver and timepieces. **Map p. 9, 1A**

## KIDS
**Aprica Kassai** Via Montenapoleone 27. Aprica Kassai makes among the world's more fashionable (and expensive) baby buggies. Check out the most outrageous ideas in the window. Feathers, anyone? **Map p. 8, 3A**

**Chicco** Piazza Diaz 2. Children's chain Chicco has become an institution among new (and expecting) Italian parents, providing all the basics for babies and older kids up to age eight. This store is immense, with a Chiccolandia playland in the basement, a great distraction device while you get on with your shopping. **Map p. 8, 2C**

**Prenatal** Corso Vittorio Emanuele II 13. Just about everything for young children, babies and mums-to-be, from clothes to prams to toys, games and books. Even if you are addicted to Mothercare, check it out. Also Corso XXII Marzo 4, Corso Buenos Aires 26, Corso Vercelli 51, Via Dante 7 and many other places throughout the city. **Map p. 9, 1B**

## MUSIC

**Messaggerie Musicali** Corso Vittorio Emanuele, corner of Galleria del Corso 2. Italy's largest music megastore, with over 4,000 m2 of compact discs, cassettes, records, books, plus T-shirts, gadgets and video games. **Map p. 8, 3C**

**Ricordi Mediastores** Galleria Vittorio Emanuele 3. If you are curious to find out what Italians are listening to, take a peek at this underground music store, located in the Galleria Vittorio Emanuele on the right hand side as you head from the Duomo. Also videos, DVDs, T-shirts and computer games. Then, if you keep going, you end up in the Feltrinelli book store. Here you can check out the magazines, of which Italy is a major producer. See especially the design and architecture offerings. **Map p. 8, 2B**

## ALSO...

### BEAUTY SUPPLIES

**Acqua di Parma** Via Gesù 3. Cologne and beauty products for men and women (including soaps and massage oils, shaving foam and talcum powder). Also cashmere dressing gowns, soft towels and caramel leather travelling bags. All purchases are exquisitely wrapped, with Parma yellow paper and thick black ribbons. **Map p. 8, 3B**

### EYEWEAR

**Solaris** Piazza Duomo 31. Designer names include Gucci, Chanel, Dior, D&G and Roberto Cavalli. Check out what RayBan, Diesel and Oakley are up to, as well. **Map p. 8, 3C**

### GLOVES

**Sermoneta Gloves** Via della Spiga 46. A good source of leather gloves and other accessories; also one of the more affordable stores in this street. **Map p. 9, 1A**

### LINGERIE

**La Perla** Via Montenapoleone 1. Lots of lingerie, sheer body suits, swimsuits, as well as ready-to-wear and coats from this Bologna-based company. This was the first La Perla boutique to open in Milan, the other is in Corso Vercelli. **Map p. 9, 1B**

# BRERA

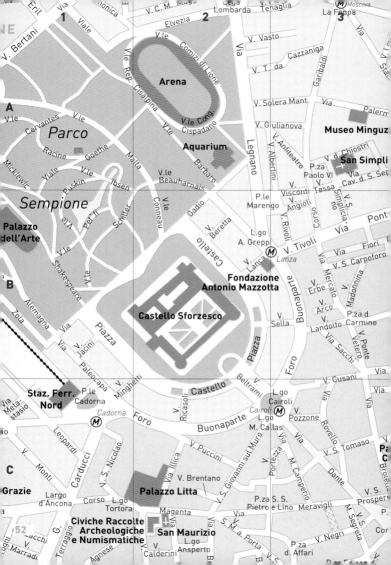

**1**

**2**

**3**

Via Parini

V. Tarchetti

V. Cavalieri

F. Turati

**Museo della Permanente**

V. Mangini

Solferino

Via

San Marco

V. S. Fermo d. Batt.

P.za S. Angelo

L.go Donegani

Moscova

Manin

**Giardi**

P.za Mirabello

V. Bertoni

V. Sandri

V. Pr. Amedeo

F. Turati

Montebello

(M) *Turati*

**A**

V. C. Porta

**Museo del Cinema**

Via Goito

Cernaia

Corso

V. M. De Marchi

V. C. Porta

**Pubblic**

**Museo Treccani**

Via

Via Fatebenefratelli

Via

Via Fiori Oscuri

Annunciata

Piazza Cavour

Via

**Civica Galleria d'Arte Moderna**

**Pinacoteca di Brera**

**Museo Astronomico**

Giardini

P.za S. Erasmo

Borgonuovo

V. dei Pisoni

Via della

Via d. Vecchio Politecnico

**Padiglion**

*Orto Botanico*

V. F. Gabba

Pieta

V. Cr. Rossari

V. Rossari

P.le Morandi

**B**

di

(M) *Montenapoleone*

Borgospesso

S. Spirito

Via della

Marina

V. S. Primo

assino one Brera

Via

Montе

V. M. Romagnosi

Via Gesu

**Palazzo del Senato**

Orso

Andegari

Via

Via Sant'Andrea

**Museo Bagatti Valsecchi**

Senato

Spiga

**Museo Poldi Pezzoli**

V. Morone

Monte

Bigli

Verri

Via S. Andrea

**Museo di Milano**

Via Bagutta

S. Damian

S. Cecilia

V. Boito

L.go De Sabata

G. Verdi

**Teatro alla Scala**

**Museo Manzoniano**

P.za Belgioioso

Napoleone

Vicolo del Duca

V. Filodrammatici

Via

P.za Scala

Case Rotte

Catena

P.za Medea

C.so

Matteotti

**San Babila**

P.za S. Babila

**C**

V. Dalmazio

S. Pellico

**Palazzo Marino**

V. Marino

P.za S. Fedele

V. Hoepli

S. Pietro all'Orto

(M) *San Babila*

Margherita

**Galleria Vittorio Emanuele II**

Via Agnello

S. Paolo

V. Borgogna

L.go Toscanini

S. Grossi

Mengoni

Foscolo

Radegonda

V. S. Raffaele

P.za Liberty

Emanuele II

Europa

**Palazzo della Ragione**

Mercanti

(M) *Duomo*

V. Berchet

Vittorio

Corso

L.go Corsia dei Servi

53

This is one of the most attractive areas of the old city, with its fine private houses, art galleries, original shops and interesting antique stores. The Brera Academy of Fine Arts transformed the district, particularly during the 1950s and 1960s, into a meeting place for artists. Today this area, still teeming with students at the academy, is popular for its bars, clubs, restaurants and nightlife, particularly on Via Fiori Chiari, Via Madonnina, Via Formentini, Via Mercato, Via Pontaccio and Via Solferino.

# Pinacoteca di Brera

| | |
|---|---|
| **OPEN** | The picture gallery is open 8.30 am–7.15 pm, Tues–Sun (last entry 45 minutes before closing). |
| **CLOSED** | Mon, 1/1, 1/5, 25/12 |
| **CHARGES** | Regular admission €5, reduced admission €2.50, under 18 or over 65 free |
| **GUIDED VISITS** | Audio guides available |
| **DISABLED ACCESS** | Yes (ask at reception) |
| **SERVICES** | Cloakroom, information desk, museum shop |
| **TELEPHONE** | General information 02 722631; reservations 02 8942 1146 |
| **WEB** | www.brera.beniculturali.it |
| **MAIN ENTRANCE** | Via Brera 28 |
| **GETTING THERE** | M2 to Lanza, M3 to Montenapoleone |

## HIGHLIGHTS
**Andrea Mantegna's *Dead Christ* and *St Luke the***      Room 6
***Evangelist*; Giovanni Bellini's *Pietà*, *Madonna Greca* and**
***Madonna and Child*; Cima da Conegliano's**
***St Peter Martyr with Saints***

Via Verdi and Via Brera lead north from La Scala to the Palazzo di Brera, a centre of the arts and sciences in Lombardy. Not only the famous picture gallery, but also the Academy of Fine Arts, the Biblioteca Nazionale (with some one million volumes, including 2,357 incunabula and 2,000 manuscripts), the Astronomical Observatory and the Institute of Science and Letters are here.

Stairs lead up from the far side of the courtyard to the loggia on the first floor and the entrance to the famous Pinacoteca di Brera, one of the best art galleries of Italy and with the finest existing collection of Northern Italian painting.

The gallery was founded in the 18th C by the Accademia di Belle Arti, and was enlarged through acquisitions and paintings from Lombard and Venetian churches before it was officially inaugurated in 1809. The collection has continued to grow in this century, with numerous donations. The gallery exhibits are attractively displayed, both chronologically and by schools, but unfortunately the collection is never shown in its entirety; some rooms are closed when there is a shortage of custodians, although scholars can ask for special permission to see them. There are long-term plans to open the adjacent Palazzo Citterio in Via Brera as an extension to the gallery to exhibit the 19th- and 20th-C works and the Jesi collection.

The Palazzo di Brera building was begun by Francesco Maria Richini in 1651 on the site of the medieval church of Santa Maria di Brera, the nave of which survives. In the monumental courtyard, by Richini, is a heroic statue in bronze of Napoleon I by Antonio Canova (a marble version of the statue is at Apsley House, London).

**ROOM 1 AND GALLERY** Beyond a small room with the self-portrait of **Francesco Hayez**, the long gallery temporarily displays early 20th-C works (particularly the Futurists) from the Jesi collection, including works by **Boccioni**, **Sironi**, **Balla**, **Severini**, **Carrà**, **Morandi**, **de Pisis**, **Rosso** and **Martini**. New acquisitions are also hung here, including a work by **Massimo Campigli**.

The chronological display begins in **ROOMS 2 AND 3** with 13th-C Italian paintings. A fine polyptych by **Gentile da Fabriano** is displayed in **ROOM 4**.

**ROOMS 5-7** These rooms contain works of the 15th- and 16th-C Venetian school. Notably, **ROOM 5** contains some masterpieces by **Mantegna**, including his famous *Lamentation Over the Dead Christ*, with its remarkable foreshortening. This sombre-toned and chilling work is also unusual for having been painted on canvas, a

# BRERA GALLERY

**Andrea Mantegna** *Lamentation Over the Dead Christ* (1490)

rare technique at the time. There are also three exquisite works by **Giovanni Bellini**: a *Pietà*, the *Madonna Greca* (one of his finest paintings) and a *Madonna and Child* in an airy landscape (1510), beautifully coloured, and painted near the end of Bellini's life. Two works by **Cima da Conegliano** include *St Peter Martyr with Saints*, with its near photographic clarity, and *Madonna and Child Enthroned*. **ROOM 7** has 16th-C Venetian portraits by **Titian**, **Lorenzo Lotto** and **Tintoretto**.

**ROOM 8** The highlight of this room is *St Mark Preaching in Alexandria*, a splendid large painting commissioned from **Gentile and Giovanni Bellini** by the Scuola Grande di San Marco in Venice. The painting is full of wonderful details, including veiled women and, in the background, a giraffe. It was begun by Gentile in 1504 and completed by Giovanni after Gentile's death. The similarity of the building and square that form the background for the crowd are a deliberate echo of Piazza San Marco in Venice.

**ROOM 9** displays 16th-C Venetian paintings, most notably **Paolo Veronese**'s *Baptism and Temptation of Christ* and **Tintoretto**'s theatrical *Finding of the Body of St Mark at Alexandria*. In this painting, St Mark's spirit stands at the left with hand upraised, stopping the Venetians in their search for his sacred body. At his feet and hanging from the raised crypts are corpses. The drama of the long hall and the placement of the figures, arrested in frantic motion, makes this painting one of the highlights of the Venetian Renaissance.

**ROOM 14** is devoted to the 16th-C Venetian school, with works by **Palma Vecchio**, **Paris Bordone** (*Baptism of Christ*), **Bonifacio Veronese**, **Giovanni Cariani**, **Giovanni Battista Moroni** and **Giovanni Gerolamo Savoldo**.

**ROOM 15** holds the anonymous *Pala Sforzesca* (showing the Madonna enthroned with Doctors of the Church and the family of Lodovico il Moro). The work, an abundant display of lavishness, with jewels and carvings and rich silks, is by an unknown Lombard painter (c. 1490–1520), known from this painting as the 'Maestro della Pala Sforzesca'. Also here is **Vincenzo Foppa**'s *Polyptych*, with its gilded frames.

**ROOM 16** The highlight of this room is **Sofonisba Anguissola**'s *Portrait of Minerva Anguissola* (after 1560).

**ROOM 18** The collection of 16th-C Lombard paintings continues, including Altobello Melone's *Portrait of Alda Gambara* and Giovanni Antonio Boltraffio's *Portrait of Gerolamo Casio*.

**ROOM 19** contains a very fine collection of paintings by followers of Leonardo da Vinci.

**ROOM 20** focuses on the 15th-C Ferrarese and Emilian schools. Here are **Francesco del Cossa**'s *St John the Baptist* and *St Peter*, two polyptych panels considered Brera masterpieces. The pictures are full of detail, from the hanging beads to the knots in

**Francesco Hayez** *The Kiss* (1895)

the saints' sandals. There is a notable vigour in the faces and strength in their bodies, both in the muscled form of St John and the thoughtful visage of St Peter.

**ROOM 21** includes polyptychs by 15th-C painters from the Marches and a delightful group of works by **Carlo Crivelli**: *Crucifixion*, *Madonna della Candeletta* (Madonna of the Candle), *Coronation of the Virgin* and *Pietà* (1483). Crivelli mixed traditional gold background with the more modern, at that time, focus on details, such as the apple at Mary's feet or the petals of the flowers in the vase (the candle itself is in the bottom left corner). Note how his subjects' bare toes grip the edge of the dais.

**ROOM 24** holds the two most famous works in the collection: **Raphael**'s *Marriage of the Virgin* (the 'Sposalizio' of 1504), painted when he was only twenty-one, and **Piero della Francesca**'s *Montefeltro Altarpiece*, with the Madonna surrounded by angels and saints. Raphael's *Marriage* is the masterpiece of his Umbrian period. The simplicity of the scene gives the picture a tranquil, almost melancholy atmosphere, as does the near emptiness of the background and the placement of the round temple, through which the viewer can see the clear blue of the uncluttered sky.

Piero della Francesca had a love of the geometries of Renaissance architecture, and this altarpiece demonstrates that affection in the perfect perspective of the angles of the vault. Kneeling before the Madonna and Child is Federigo, Duke of Montefeltro, who commissioned the piece; hanging in the back from a massive seashell is a famous detail, the mysterious opaque sphere long thought to be an ostrich egg, but now considered to be possibly a pearl, since in Marian literature Jesus is described as forming like a pearl in Mary's womb.

Also displayed here is a processional standard, an early work by **Luca Signorelli**, painted on both sides with the *Flagellation* and *Madonna and Child*, and *Christ at the Column* (from Chiaravalle), the only known panel painting by **Donato Bramante**.

**ROOM 28** displays works of the 17th-C Bolognese school, including **Federico Barocci**'s *Martyrdom of St Vitalis*, in which

Mannerist styles give way to a forceful naturalism. The turbulence of Barocci's painting is in contrast to the simple, yet dramatic *Saints Peter and Paul* by **Guido Reni**. Unlike most paintings of saintly figures, here there is no ornamentation; the saints are robed simply in orange or red rendered in intense colour against a dark background and brooding sky.

**ROOM 29** highlights **Caravaggio** and his followers. Caravaggio's *Supper at Emmaus* concentrates, with tremendous emotion, on the faces of the watchers and the half-shadowed Christ. One of Caravaggio's followers was **Orazio Gentileschi**, whose *Martyrs Valerian, Tiburtius and Cecilia Visited by an Angel* is a splendidly large painting with a formal power.

**ROOM 23** has portraits by **Rembrandt** (of his sister) and **Anthony Van Dyck**, and works by **Brueghel the Elder**.

**ROOM 33** displays 16th- and 17th-C Flemish and Dutch paintings including works by the 'Maestro di Anversa' (1518), a triptych by Jan de Beer, and a *St Francis* by **El Greco**.

**ROOM 34** The highlight of this room is **Giuseppe Maria Crespi**'s *Crucifixion*, in which the artist's masterful use of light creates an atmosphere of intense emotion and drama.

**ROOMS 37 AND 38** hold 19th-C works, including **Francesco Hayez**'s *The Kiss* (see picture on p. 60), his most famous work, in which the young man's tipped hat nearly, but not quite, hides the passionate kiss itself. Also in this room is Silvestro Lega's *Pergolato*, which wonderfully creates a sense of summer heat with the patches of light and colour around the subjects, the haze of the sky in the distance, and the women's languid gestures.

**ROOM 38** The second version (1895-1897) of Giuseppe Pellizza da Volpedo's famous *Quarto Stato* and **Boccioni**'s *Self-Portrait* hang just before the exit. Pelizza worked on *Quarto Stato* for altogether ten years before he was satisfied with the result.

# Castello Sforzesco

## MUSEO D'ARTE ANTICA, MUSEO DELLE ARTI DECORATIVE E STRUMENTI MUSICALI, PINACOTECA AND RACCOLTA STAMPE BERTARELLI E ARCHIVIO FOTOGRAFICO

**OPEN**
The musuems are open 9 am–5.30 pm, Tues–Sun, except the Raccolta Bertarelli e Archivio Fotografico, which is open 9 am–12.30 pm, Mon–Fri.

**CLOSED**
*Raccolta Bertarelli e Archivio Fotografico* Sat-Sun
*Other Museums* Mon, 1/1, 1/5, 25/12

**CHARGES**
Admission is free to the castle. Museum admission is €3/1.50.

**GUIDED VISITS**
Audio guides; English-language guide available by Ad Artem at 02 659 8885.

**DISABLED ACCESS**
Yes (ask at Reception); there is a lift in the Cortile della Rocchetta

**SERVICES**
Bookshop

**TELEPHONE**
*Museo d'Arte Antica* 02 8846 3703, 02 8646 3054
*Museo delle Arti Decorative e Strumenti Musicali* 02 8846 3666, 02 874546
*Pinacoteca* 02 884 3703, 02 8646 3054
*Raccolta Stampe Bertarelli e Archivio Fotografico* 02 8846 3836
*Civiche Raccolte Archeologiche e Numismatiche* 02 7200 2128

**WEB**
www.milanocastello.it

**MAIN ENTRANCE**
*Castello Sforzesco* Foro Bonaparte
*Museo d'Arte Antica* Corte Ducale, ground floor
*Pinacoteca* Corte Ducale, first floor
*Museo di Arte Decorative e Strumenti Musicali* Corte Ducale, first floor and Rocchetta
*Raccolta Stampe Berarelli e Archivio Fotografico* On either side of the Torre del Filarete
*Civiche Raccolte Archeologiche e Numismatiche* Corte Ducale, basement

**GETTING THERE**
M1 to Cordusio, M2 Lanza/Cadorna

**The Castello Sforzesco stands firm at the meeting place of the spacious Foro Buonaparte, Largo Cairoli and the green Piazza Castello. The Castello was a stronghold built in 1451–66 for**

Francesco Sforza, a mercenary who rose to become Duke of Milan (it was originally the site of a 14th-C castle of the Visconti). After a long period of use as barracks, the Castello was restored at the turn of the 19th C by Luca Beltrami (1893–1904). Badly damaged by bombing in 1943, when two-thirds of the archives and many other treasures were lost, it was carefully restored, and now contains important art collections and cultural institutions.

## THE BUILDING

The fortress is square in plan, with three towers on the façade. The entrance to the castle from Largo Cairoli is beneath the tower that gives access to the huge Cortile d'Armi, the main courtyard. Almost in the centre of the far side is the 15th-C Torre di Bona di Savoia, beyond which, to the left, is the Rocchetta, which served as a keep. On the right is the Corte Ducale, the residential part of the castle built in 1472, with a charming courtyard.

# MUSEO D'ARTE ANTICA

The Museo d'Arte Antica covers twelve hundred years of Lombard, Italian and European sculpture, from the 4th to the 16th C, displayed in the magnificent halls where Milan's dukes once held court. The installation was designed by the architects of Studio BBPR in 1956.

## HIGHLIGHTS

| | |
|---|---|
| Bonino da Campione's *Bernabò Visconti Equestrian Monument* | Section I |
| Bambaia's *Tomb of Gaston de Foix* Michelangelo's *Rondanini Pietà* | Section IV |

**SECTION I** EARLY CHRISTIAN, ROMANESQUE AND GOTHIC SCULPTURE

In the first four rooms are important **fragments from ancient churches** and other Byzantine and Romanesque remains,

**Castello Sforzesco**

including a 6th-C marble portrait head supposedly of the Empress Theodora. Also worth a look are Visconti tombs by Bonino da Campione (1363); remains of the façade of Santa Maria di Brera and statues from the east gate of the city. All lie under the watchful eye of **Bonino da Campione**'s marble *Bernabò Visconti Equestrian Monument (1363)*, which stands with massive presence above a columned sarcophagus. The rider was once painted, and had golden spurs and shield, but now sits in austere dignity made all the more impressive by the fierce expression of his face.

**SECTION II** THE COMMUNE OF MILAN AND THE SPANISH OCCUPATION

In the *east wing*, beyond a small chapel with 14th-C Venetian sculpture, are works from Milan's communal and Spanish periods. The first room contains 12th-C reliefs from the old Porta Romana, showing the triumph of the Milanese over Barbarossa (1176).

The *Sala delle Asse*, at the northeast corner of the castle, has remarkable frescoed decoration in the vault, designed in 1498 by **Leonardo da Vinci** but subsequently repainted. Branches and

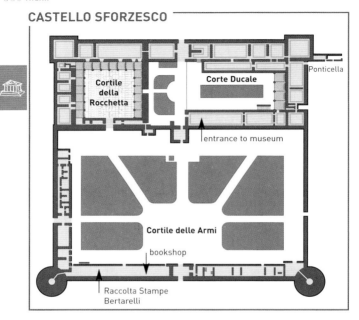

## CASTELLO SFORZESCO

leaves are used in a complicated architectural structure in which the form of the octagon recurs. On the far wall are two fascinating fragments of monochrome tempera decoration by the hand of Leonardo (1498), depicting tree trunks with branches and roots growing out of cracks in stratified rock formations. Off the *Sala delle Asse* are the two small rooms of the *Ponticella*, a bridge over the moat built by Bramante.

**SECTION III** LOMBARD RENAISSANCE AND ARMOURY
The north wing of the *Corte Ducale* displays **15th-C Lombard sculptures** in rooms that retain some of their original decoration. The *Sala dei Ducali* is decorated with coats of arms showing the ancestry of Galeazzo Maria Sforza; the *Sala delle Colombine*, on the

right, has red-and-gold fresco decorations with the arms of Bona di Savoia; and the long *Sala Verde*, originally the ballroom, is divided by Renaissance doorways salvaged from Milanese palaces.

**SECTION IV** BAMBAIA AND MICHELANGELO

You'll recognize the *Sala degli Scarlioni* immediately from its red and white, zigzag decoration. Here are the museum's two most famous works: the effigy by **Bambaia** of Gaston de Foix, a French general who died in battle in Ravenna in 1512, and the *Rondanini Pietà*, the unfinished last work of **Michelangelo** named after the palace in Rome where it used to be displayed. The 89-year-old sculptor worked at intervals on this emotionally charged statue during the last nine years of his life, and even six days before his death. According to Vasari, he reused a block of marble in which he had already roughed out a *Pietà* with a different design and a smaller scale. The work departs from the usual form of the Pietà, with Jesus reclining across Mary's knees, and is thought to have been made not on commission, but for the artist's own enjoyment.

From the corner a wooden bridge leads out into the *Corte Ducale* across a subterranean court with a 16th-C fountain.

# MUSEO DELLE ARTI DECORATIVE E STRUMENTI MUSICALI

The 'Municipal Museum of Decorative Arts and Musical Instruments' is the most important applied arts museum in Lombardy, occupying four rooms of the private apartments on the first floor of the Corte Ducale as well as the upper floors of the tower known as the Rochetta. It is reached by the external staircase beneath the Loggia Ducale.

## HIGHLIGHTS

**Frescoed room from the Castgello di Roccabianca**

Furniture collection

**Belgiojoso collection of 17th-C Flemish and Dutch paintings**

| | |
|---|---|
| **Spinet played by Mozart**<br>**Musical manuscripts** | Instrument collection |
| **18th-C dinner services** | Ceramics collection |
| **Women's accessories,**<br>**especially shoes and fans** | Costume and<br>fashion collection |

The *Corte Ducale* rooms contain a splendid collection of furniture, with Lombard interiors of the 15th–18th centuries arranged chronologically. This section also holds the Belgiojoso collection of 17th-C Flemish and Dutch paintings, including a monochrome sketch of three female figures and putti by **Rubens**.

The great *Sala Verde Superiore* was the scene for a dazzling feast and spectacle (the *Festa del Paradiso*) organized for the Sforza by **Leonardo da Vinci** in 1490, to mark the marriage of Gian Galeazzo and Isabella of Aragon. Leonardo's design was described by contemporary sources as a masterpiece of invention, with a revolving stage and an allegorical tableau of the Zodiac.

To reach the *Rocchetta* rooms, climb the stairs at the entrance to the Museo d'Arte Antica and walk down a corridor inside the castle walls—look through the slits to see the *Piazza d'Armi*, *Corte Ducale* and *Rocchetta*.

The splendid large **collection of musical instruments** on the first floor of the Rochetta features a fine assortment of lutes and string instruments, including a beautiful guitar of 1624 and the pocket-sized viols known as pochettes. There is an outstanding group of wind instruments (notably delicately carved ivory and bone hunting horns) and a rich collection of musical manuscripts and autographs, but one of the main draws for visitors is a spinet played by the 14-year-old Mozart.

The aisled ball court is hung with tapestries of the showing the months from designs by **Bramantino** (c. 1503); the tapestries were commissioned after the expulsion of the Sforza by the French marshal Gian Giacomo Trivulzio. January has two faces—one young, the other old and bearded, like the god Janus—and holds the key to the new year.

The second floor displays a large collection of Italian and foreign **ceramics**. Highlights include *ceramiche sgraffite*, common in

Emilia in the 14th and 15th centuries, on which an incision made before firing allows the raw red terracotta to underscore the design in mineral colours such as yellow and green. Also important are the collections of Italian Renaissance majolica; complete dinner services of 18th-C Milanese and Lombard manufacture, showing the pastoral designs and chinoiserie typical of the time; and early coffee cups from Venetian cafés.

Selections from the museum's extensive collections of **costume and fashion** and **Islamic, Coptic and European textiles** are shown on a rotating basis. There are also displays of glass, goldsmiths' work, enamels, ivories, church silver, and scientific instruments (including a geometric compass designed by Galileo in 1606) and small bronzes.

## PINACOTECA

The Pinacoteca, also on the first floor of the *Corte Ducale*, displays Italian painting of the 13th–18th centuries, with special emphasis on Lombard and Venetian masters. The gallery has some of the best works of locals such as **Foppa**, **Bergognone** and **Bramantino**, and works by 'outsiders' like **Mantegna**, **Antonello da Messina**, **Correggio**, **Lotto**, **Titian** and **Canaletto**, but only 240 of the fifteen hundred works in the collection are displayed in the Pinacoteca's seven rooms.

The Pinacoteco's **Belgiojoso collection of Flemish paintings** and the Roccabianca frescoes are displayed in the Museum of Decorative Arts. The installation, with the paintings on mobile supports connected to the ceiling, was created in 1980 by the architects Albini, Helb and Piva; it succeeds the 1956 arrangement of Studio BBPR. Like the Museum of Decorative Arts, the Pinacoteca is reached by the external staircase beneath the Loggia Ducale.

## HIGHLIGHTS

| | |
|---|---|
| Andrea Mantegna's *Madonna Trivulzio* | Room 20 |
| Giovanni Bellini's *Madonna and Child* | |
| Giovanni Antonio's *Boltraffio's Lady in Red* | Room 25 |
| Lorenzo Lotto's *Boy Holding a Book of Petrarch* | |
| Antony van Dyck's *Henrietta Maria of France* | |

**ROOM 20** In the vaulted *Torre Falconara*, the former bedchamber of the Dukes of Milan, are some beautiful Late Gothic and Quattrocento works, including the expressive *Madonna Trivulzio* by **Mantegna** (signed and dated 1497 on the music sheet held by the singing angel at the centre). There is also a superb *Madonna and Child* by **Giovanni Bellini** and a very unusual work (the *Madonna of Humility*) by **Fra Filippo Lippi**. The tower's name comes from the hunting falcons that were kept on the top floor.

**ROOMS 21–24** cover Lombard Renaissance, Mannerist and Counter Reformation painting. The Renaissance in Lombardy is represented primarily by **Vincenzo Foppa** (*Madonna del libro*, *Martyrdom of St Sebastian*), **Bergognone** (*St Benedict*) and **Bramantino** (*Noli me tangere*, a fresco from the former church of Santa Maria del Giardino).

The passage from the Mannerist to the Baroque of the Counter Reformation can be traced through two paintings (*Santa Tecla*, *San Vittore*) by **Pellegrino Tibaldi**, the favourite painter of St Charles Borromeo, the Milanese cardinal and archbishop who was one of the most important figures of the Counter Reformation in Italy.

**ROOM 25** contains a magnificent display of portraits by **Giovanni Bellini**, **Correggio**, **Tintoretto**, **Titian** and others, including **Giovanni Antonio Boltraffio**'s *Lady in Red*. A native Milanese, Boltraffio was one of the many that were deeply impressed with Leonardo da Vinci, who had a huge effect on painting in Milan in the years he spent there. There is also a fine portrait (*Boy Holding a Book of Petrarch*) by the idiosyncratic, restless **Lorenzo Lotto**. *Henrietta Maria of France*, by **Anthony van Dyck**, is one of some 35 portraits the painter made of the melancholy queen, consort to the doomed English king Charles I.

**ROOM 26** continues with 17th- and 18th-C Lombard and Italian painting.

## RACCOLTA STAMPE BERTARELLI E ARCHIVIO FOTOGRAFICO

Milan's collections of prints and photographs began as the private collection of Achille Bertarelli, a Milanese lawyer who lived at the end of the 19th C. Now the collection holds over one million prints, including works by old masters, such as **Mantegna**, **Dürer**, **Canaletto**, **Piranesi**, **Hogarth** and **Tiepolo**, as well as modern masters like **Munch**, **Boccioni**, **Giacometti** and **Morandi**.

The photographic archive also includes the collection of Luca Beltrami, with over 300,000 images that trace the development of Milan over the last century and a half. There is also a laboratory that sells prints from antique negatives.

## SECTIONS OF THE CIVICHE RACCOLTE ARCHEOLOGICHE E NUMISMATICHE

Three sections of the Civiche Raccolte Archeologiche e Numismatiche (see p. 111) are also displayed in the castle. From the *Corte Ducale* you descend to a basement room with the epigraphic section, which includes Roman inscriptions on public life, religious life, trade and private family life.

In the arcaded courtyard of the *Rocchetta*, in the design of which both Filarete and Bramante had a hand, is the entrance to the **Egyptian section**, also in the basement. It contains a small collection of objects dating from the Old Kingdom to the age of Ptolemy. Also off the courtyard is the entrance to the prehistoric section, which includes a room containing material from Lombardy that dates from the late Bronze Age to the Roman period.

# in the area

**Museo Astronomico** (Via Brera 28; M1 to Cairoli, M2 to Lanza; 02 805 7309; open 9 am–4.30 pm, Mon-Fri). The Palazzo di Brera is home to Milan's oldest active research institute, the Astronomical Observatory, established in 1765. Historical instruments are displayed in the observatory museum. The Istituto di Fisica Generale Applicata of Milan University organizes guided visits, multimedia shows and direct observations of the night sky through the 19th-C telescope that Giovanni

Virginio Schiaparelli (1835-1910) used to observe Mars and make his famous maps of the Red Planet. Schiaparelli's maps are just one of the important advances made here; others include the calculation of the orbit of Uranus (1783-84) and one of the first geodetic map studies. One of the original observation domes (Cupola Schiaparelli), built in 1862 to house the 22-cm Merz reflector, is still used for demonstrations. The Observatory's scientists are actively involved in the research programme of the Galileo National Telescope at La Palma, Canary Islands, and in the design and implementation of orbital telescopes. **Map p. 53, 1B**

### *Teatro alla Scala*

**Map p. 8, 2B** The Teatro alla Scala is Italy's most famous opera house. Built for Empress Maria Theresa of Austria, in 1776, on the site of the church of Santa Maria della Scala, it opened in 1778 with *Europa Riconosciuta* by Antonio Salieri and Mattia Verazi. Works by Rossini, Donizetti, Bellini, Verdi and Puccini were first performed here. From the beginning of the 20th C it was conducted by the great Arturo Toscanini. Because of his opposition to Facism, he moved to the US in 1938, but led the orchestra again in 1946 when the building was reopened.

For the 2002-2005 seasons, while the main theatre undergoes renovation, the Teatro alla Scala has been transferred to the new Teatro degli Arcimboldi, built by the Municipality of Milan in collaboration with Pirelli on a design by Studio Gregotti Associati International.

The Museo Teatrale alla Scala has moved for the period to new quarters in Palazzo Busca (Map p. 98, 1B; Corso Magenta 71; 9 am–6 pm, Tue–Sun; 02 805 3418).

**Orto Botanico** (Via Brera 28; M1 to Cairoli, M2 to Lanza; 02 8901 0419; open Mon–Fri by appointment) Maria Theresa of Austria established a chair in medicinal botany at Brera in 1774, creating the Hortus Botanicus Braidensis so that students could observe and experiment directly with nature. The garden was designed by Giuseppe Piermarini and by Fulgenzio Vitman, its first director. Their 18th-C design survives in the elliptical pools. Today the garden is known for its historic plants, notably two large examples of *Ginkgo biloba* (one male, one female) and a great *Pterocaya caucasica*. **Map p. 53, 1B**

**Via Borgonuovo** This elegant street, with a series of fine palaces and courtyards, lies directly behind the Brera palace. You can get there by taking Via Fiori Oscuri, named after the brothels here that featured brunettes (*fiori oscuri* means dark flowers; blondes, or *fiori chiari*, worked on the block west of Via Brera). Palazzo Moriggia, at Via Borgonuovo 23, was rebuilt in the 18th C by Piermarini. Today it houses the Museo del Risorgimento (open 9 am–1 pm, 2 pm–5.30 pm, Tues–Sun; 02 8846 4170), which covers the process of Italy's unification, from the arrival of Napoleon in Lombardy in 1796 up to the taking of Rome in 1870. **Map p. 53, 1B**

**Museo Minguzzi** (Via Palermo 11; open 10 am–1 pm and 3 pm–6 pm, Tue-Sun, admission €6; 02 805 1460) This little museum, dedicated to the work of the 20th-C Milanese sculptor Luciano Minguzzi, is located just a few paces from the Palazzo di Brera, in an interesting old ice house overlooking a small court. Minguzzi is known primarily for his public art projects (he did a set of cathedral doors and the Carabinieri monument in Milan, the *Doors of Good and Evil* at St Peter's in Rome, and the statue of Pope John Paul II in Krakow). **Map p. 52, 3A**

**San Simpliciano** This northernmost of Milan's early Christian basilicas is dedicated to St Ambrose's successor in the episcopal chair. It was probably founded by St Ambrose himself in the 4th C and, despite alterations of the 12th C, stands largely in its original form, with eighteen huge window embrasures revealed after 1945. The interior contains the *Coronation of the Virgin*, a fine fresco by Bergognone, in the restored Romanesque apse masked by the towering altar. **Map p. 52, 3A**

**Parco Sempione** This large park begins on the far side of the Castello Sforzesco on the site of a 15th-C ducal park. The **Palazzo dell'Arte** (Map p. 52, 1B; open 10 am–8 pm, Tue-Sun, 02 724 341), built in 1931–33 by Giovanni Muzio, has recently been restored as an important exhibition centre. It is the historic seat of the Triennale di Milano, a worldwide survey of architecture and industrial design established in 1923 and still considered one of the most important appointments on the calendar of architects, designers and furniture makers. Contemporary architects Gae Aulenti and Michele de Lucchi are responsible for the state-of-the art Galleria della Triennale and the adjoining public areas on the ground floor.

  **The Aquarium**, in a fine Art Nouveau building of 1906 (**Map p. 52, 2A;** open 9 am–5.30 pm, Tues–Sun; 02 864 2051), with fine decorations on the exterior, has marine and freshwater fish and important study collections. The **Arena (Map p. 53, 2A)** was first built by Luigi Canonica in

**A stand at the international furniture fair, 2004**

1806–07, but the 110-m aluminium tower was erected in 1933 by Giò Ponti and Cesare Chiodi. At the far end of the park is the **Arco della Pace** (**Map p. 53, 1A**). A triumphal arch modelled on the Arch of Severus in Rome and built by Luigi Cagnola in 1807–38, it was begun in honour of Napoleon I, but was dedicated instead to Peace by Ferdinand I of Austria on its completion. It marks the beginning of the Corso Sempione, part of the 182-km historic Simplon Road, constructed by order of Napoleon from Geneva to Sesto Calende across the Simplon Pass (1800–05).

**Fondazione Antonio Mazzotta** (Foro Bonaparte 50; M1 Cairoli and M2 Lanza; open 10 am–7.30 pm, Mon–Weds and Fri–Sun, and 10 am–10.30 pm, Tue and Thur; admission €6.20; 02 878 197). The Fondazione Mazzotta was established in 1988 to preserve a private collection of works on paper (by Goya, Modigliani, Boccioni, Kandinsky, Matisse, Warhol), Art Nouveau glass (including Gallé, Tiffany and Daum vases) and rare books. These items are not usually on view, however, as the foundation's limited space is used to present changing exhibitions of modern art and industrial design. Past 'guests' have included Gustav Klimt, Otto Dix, Die Brücke, Federico Fellini and Nobel Prize dramatist Dario Fo. **Map p. 53, 2B**

# commercial galleries

**Anfiteatro Arte** Via Anfiteatro 9, 02 8645 8549, fax 02 8645 8549, e-mail: galleriaanfiteatro@libero.it. European modern masters, blue-chip and fashionable younger artists: Vanessa Beecroft, Alighiero Boetti, Christo, Lucio Fontana, Hans Hartung, Anselm Kiefer, Jannis Kounellis, Mimmo Rotella, Mario Schifano and Antonio Tàpies. **Map p. 8, 1A**

**Arte Centro** Via dell'Annunciata 31, 02 2900 0071, fax 02 659 2631, www.lattuadastudio.it. Afro, Roberto Marcello Baldessari, Giacomo Balla, Giuseppe Capogrossi, Fortunato Depero, Gerardo Dottori, Lucio Fontana, Vasily Kandinskij, Fausto Melotti, Enrico Prampolini, Mauro Reggiani, Manlio Rho, Mimmo Rotella, Giulio Turcato, Luigi Veronesi. **Map p. 53, 2B**

**Cafiso** Piazza San Marco 1, 02 654864 or 657 0211, fax 02 659 6546, e-mail: cafisogalleriaarte@tiscalinet.it. Enrico Baj, Massimo Campigli, Domenico Cantatore, Marc Chagall, Giorgio De Chrico, Filippo De Pisis, Renato Guttuso, Asger Jorn, Mauro Reggiani, Ottone Rosai, Aligi Sassu, pio Semeghini, Mario Sironi, Arturo Tosi, Mario Tozzi. **Map p. 8, 2A**

**Salvatore + Carolina** Ala Via Monte di Pietà 1, 02 890 0901, fax 02 8646 7384, e-mail: ala@iol.it. International contemporary art. **Map p. 53, 1B**

**Cardi** Piazza Sant'Erasmo 3, 02 2900 3235, fax 02 2900 3382; Corso di Porta Nuova 38, 02 6269 0945, fax 02 6269 4016, www.galleriacardi.com. European and American top artists: Donald Baechler, Bertozzi & Casoni, Nicola De Maria, Graham Gillmore, Peter Halley, Guillermo Kuitca, Jonathan Lasker, Malcolm Morley, Vik Muniz, Not Vital, Tom Sachs, David Salle, Julian Schnabel, Philip Taaffe, Andy Warhol. **Map p. 53, 2B**

**Paolo Curti/Annamaria Gambuzzi** Via Pontaccio 19, 02 8699 8170, fax 02 7209 4052, www.paolocurti.com. Miguel Barcelo, Francesco Clemente, Enzo Cucchi, Flavio Favelli, Torben Giehler, Michael Joo, Carsten Nicolai, Erik Parker, Franco Vaccari, Dan Walsh, Andy Warhol. **Map p. 52, 3B**

**Fonte d'Abisso** Via del Carmine 7, 02 860313. European modern masters and blue-chip artists. **Map p. 52, 3B**

**Claudia Gian Ferrari** Via Fiori Oscuri 3, 02 8646 1690, fax 02 801019, ww.claudiagianferrari.com. Enrica Borghi, Lawrence Carroll, Felice Casorati, Giorgio De Chrico, Filippo De Pisis, Angelo Filomeno, Elke Krystufek, Martin Maloney, Arturo Martini, Piero Marussig, Claudio Parmiggiani, Faustro Pirandello, Mario Sironi, Hiroshi Sugito, Arturo Tosi. **Map p. 53, 1B**

**Grossetti** Via Paolo Sarpi 44, 02 3453 7186, fax 02 3453 5765, e-mail: grossettiart@tiscalinet.it. European blue-chip and cutting-edge contemporary artists: Antonio Calderara, Roberto Caracciolo, Walter Cascio, Enzo Castagno, Dadamaino, Marco Gastini, Paolo Icaro, Carmen Gloria Morales, Maria Morganti, Roberto Rizzo, Sean Shanahan, Giuseppe Spagnulo, Michael Wesely. **Map p. 53, 2A**

**Il Castello** Via Brera 16, 02 862913, fax 02 877962, e-mail: amconteilcastello@tin.it. Enrico Baj, Alighiero Boetti, Alfonso Bonavita, Alberto Burri, Carlo Carrà, Piero Dorazio, Gianni Dova, Walter Lazzaro, Fernand Léger, Ennio Morlotti, Arnaldo Pomodoro, Giulio Turcato. **Map p. 53, 1B**

**Il Mappamondo** Via Borgonuovo 2, 02 2900 2435, fax 02 2906 1971, www.ilmappamondo.com. Karel Appel, Alberto Burri, Felice Casorati, Giorgio De Chrico, Lucio Fontana, Fernand Léger, Giorgio Morandi, Serge Poliakoff, Jean-Paul Riopelle, Alberto Savinio. **Map p. 53, 1B**

**Marella** Via Lepontina 8, 02 69311460, fax 02 60730280, www.marellart.com. Off the map. Cutting-edge contemporary art: Daryoush Asgar, Eelco Brand, Chanschatz, Stephen Ellis, Luca Francesconi, Cristina Graziani, Wei Li, Terry Rodgers, He Sen, Andres Serrano, Tiehai Zhou, Adrian Tranquilli, Wuingsong Wang, Quattara Watts, Fen Weng.

**Photology** Via Moscova 25, 2 6595285, fax 02 654284, www.photology.com. Milan's premier venue for contemporary photography: Giacomo Costa, Ron Galella, Lauren Greenfield, Kurt Markus, Jack Pierson, Andres Serrano, Paul Thuile. **Map p. 52, 1C**

**Poleschi** Foro Buonaparte 68, 02 869 97153/8699 7098, fax 02 877339, www.poleschiarfte.com. European modern masters and blue-chip contemporary artists: Arman, Max Bill, Alighiero Boetti, Agostino Bonalumi, Francesco Clemente, Gino De Dominicis, Nicola De Maria, Alberto Giacometti, Sandro Martini, Aldo Mondino, Ennio Morlotti, Mimmo Paladino, Mario Sironi, Tancredi, Giuliano Vangi. **Map p. 52, 3B**

**Lia Rumma** Via Solferino 44, 02 2900 0101, fax 02 2900 3805, www.gallerialiarumma.it. Marina Abramovic, Vanessa Beecroft, Alberto Burri, Encrico Castellani, Clegg & Guttmann, Grenville Davey, Gino De Dominicis, Günther Förg, Andreas Gursky, Peter Halley, Keith Haring, Mimmo Jodice, Donald Judd, Ilya Kabakov, Andreas Karayan, William Kentridge, Anselm Kiefer, Joseph Kosuth, Robert Longo, Reinhard Mucha, Julian Opie, Gianni Piacentino, Michelangelo Pistoleoo, Aldo Rossi, Thomas Ruff, Kenny Scharf, Cindy Sherman, Haim Steinbach, Christopher Williams. **Map p. 53, 1A**

**Seno** Via Ciovasso 11, 02 86463908. International contemporary art. **Map p. 52, 3B**

**Zonca & Zonca** Via Ciovasso 4, 02 7200 3377, fax 02 7200 3369, www.zoncaezonca.com. Nobuyoshi Araki, Alighiero Boetti, Enrico Castellani, Gino De Dominicis, Nicola De Maria, Piero Dorazio, Lucio Fontana, Jan Knap, Piero Manzoni, Michelangelo Pistoletto, Mimmo Rotella, Salvo, Mario Schifano, Cy Twombly. **Map p. 52, 3B**

**Maurizio Cannavacciuolo** *Ritratto di gentiluomo i un interno* (1998) Galleria Cardi

# eat

## RESTAURANTS

€    **Trattoria degli Orti** Via Monviso 13, 02 3310 1800. Off the map; you'll need to take a taxi. The name reflects the fact that not that long ago, this area was open fields where vegetables were grown (*orti* means 'gardens'). It's out of the way, but well worth the taxi ride to get to this small, family-run trattoria in a 19th-C building. The Beduschi family have been offering simple dishes in the Venetian and Emilian traditions since 1999. There's just the one dining room,

**Installation at the international office furniture fair, 2004**

so non-smokers beware, and if you don't want the menu recited to you as is traditional, ask for a written copy. Reservations essential. Closed Sundays, three weeks in Aug and between Christmas and New Year's. No credit cards.

€€ **La Libera** Via Palermo 21, 02 805 3603. Traditional Italian seasonal cuisine (including delicious pasta and pizza), also steaks and fish. **Map p. 52, 3A**

**Torre di Pisa** Via Fiori Chiari 21, 02 874 877. People come for the Tuscan specialities in this trattoria, and it has a faithful following. Closed Sundays, Sat lunchtime, three weeks in Aug. Reservations essential. **Map p. 52, 3B**

€€€**Alfredo Gran San Bernardo** Via Borgese 14, 02 331 9000. Off the map. You'll have to get here by taxi—it's quite close to the Trattoria degli Orti (see above). It's known especially for risotto and other dishes typical of Milanese cuisine. Reservations essential. Closed Sundays, August and Dec–Jan.

**Il Sambuco** Via Messina 10, 02 3361 0333. Off the map, but close to Parco Sempione, to the north. At this restaurant attached to the Hotel Hermitage, fish is a speciality. Try their super-light *fritto misto*—fried seafod has never tasted this good. Closed Sundays, Sat lunchtime, all of Aug and Dec 25–Jan 6.

## FOR FUN

€ **Latteria San Marco** Via San Marco 24, 02 659 7653. With just ten tables to accommodate a maximum of 25 guests, the Latteria is tiny—and very popular, so you'll have to a wait for a table. It's hard to spot in a street with a number of handsome antique shops. It's on the left, as you come from Via Solferino. No credit cards. Closed Sat, Sun, all of Aug and Dec 25–Jan 6. **Map p. 53, 1A**

# WINE BARS

€ **Arcadia Tavola e Vini** Via Ponte Vetero 13. Great selection of wines as well as warm and cold snacks. **Map p. 52, 3B**

**Cotti** Via Solferino 42. A very professional place with a long tradition, original furnishings from the 1930s and a wide selection of wines and spirits. It's open late. Closed Sundays, Mondays and all of Aug. **Map p. 53, 1A**

## CAFÉS

**€**   **Giamaica** Via Brera 32. A bit down at heel these days, but frequented in the 1960s by all the leading Milan-based artists, writers, actors and musicians. The café also hosts occasional local art exhibits. **Map p. 53, 1B**

# shop

## CLOTHING

**Alecca Carrano** Via Fiori Chiari 26. It's located in the courtyard, so Alecca Carrano's store specialising in hand-made shawls for all seasons takes a bit of seeking out. The shawls range from silk to the finest wool, plain or hand-embroidered. **Map p. 52, 3B**

**Antonia** Via Ponte Vetero 2. Antonia Giacinti's selection of the best of the season's offerings includes models from top designers such as Dolce&Gabbana, Yves Saint-Laurent, Valentino, Stella McCartney, Balenciaga, Alessandro dell'Acqua, Missoni, Cruciani, Emilio Pucci and Ungaro. **Map p. 52, 3B**

**Atribu** Corso Garibaldi 49, corner of Via Anfiteatro. A feature of this highly eclectic area for the last twelve years, Atribu offers handmade clothing and accessories in exquisite fabrics such as silk, cashmere and tweed with period embroidery details. **Map p. 52, 3A**

**Bipa** Via Ponte Vetero 10. Current collections of women's clothing and shoes by Anna Molinari, Chloé, Les Tropeziennes, Nokita. Moschino Cheap&Chic and others. **Map p. 52, 3B**

**Cavalli e Nastri** Via Brera 2. Vintage fashion from the turn of the century through to the 1970s, with plenty of designer names— some reasonably priced, some not. Also a wide variety of shoes and accessories. **Map p. 53, 1B**

**Martino Midali** Via Ponte Vetero 9. Richly textured knitwear for all seasons, as well as tailored and more casual clothing including some roomier styles under the Midali Toujours label. If you are around for a few days, you might want to check out the out-of-the-way Midali outlet (it's called Affari) on the corner of Via Bronzetti and Via Marcona. See p. 95 for more. **Map p. 52, 3B**

# ANTIQUES

**Spazio 900** Corso Garibaldi 42, 02 72001775. This is the place to come for what the Italians call *modernariato*, things produced since the 1950s—called that to distinguish it from *antiquariato*. And there's a lot of *modernariato* here, including furniture, lighting and accessories from leading companies such as Cassina, Artemide, Flos and Arteluce, as well as items by Ettore Sottsass, Enzo Mari, Achille Castiglioni, Gaetano Pesce, Joe Colombo and Marco Zanuso. Open 3.30 pm–7.30 pm, Mon–Sat. **Map p. 52, 3A**

**Franco Sabatelli** Via Fiori Chiari 5. Milan's premier specialist in the restoration and sale of antique picture frames also has furniture and *objets d'art* for sale. Stroll through Via Fiori Chiari and you will see several other interesting antique shops—keep an eye out for Italian Rationalist designs from the 1920s and 1930s. **Map p. 52, 3B**

# ACCESSORIES

**Antonia Accessori** Via Ponte Vetero 1, corner of Via Cusani. If you like Antonia Giacinti's take on fashion, then check out her hand-picked accessories, too. In this lovely, light-filled space, Antonia has on offer shoes and bags from Gucci, Yves Saint-Laurent, Balenciaga, Jimmy Choo, Brian Atwood, René Caovilla, Emilio Pucci, Marc Jacobs, Valentino, Zanotti, Christian Louboutin, Pierre Hardy and Versace. **Map p. 52, 3B**

**FrancescaTrezzi** Corso Garibaldi 44. Francesca Trezzi is a young Milan-based designer, and this is her first boutique. As well as shoes and bags, she has created an intriguing collection that enables you to coordinate with your pet. **Map p. 52, 3A**

Check out the rest of Corso Garibaldi while you are here—it stretches from Via Mercato right the way to Piazza XXV Aprile (at the other side of which is Corso Como). There are a lot of shops, bars and interesting things to look at in this recently gentrified part of town, which exemplifies how Brera has changed in recent years.

## THE HOME

**Creso Gallery** Corso Garibaldi 77. You may not buy anything, but you will surely enjoy looking at these exquisitely designed items for the home. On second thoughts, you probably will want to take something away, if only to remind you of the experience. **Map p. 52, 3A**

**Docks Dora** Viale Crispi 7, on the corner of Via Varese. If this looks like a clothing store, well, it is. But, besides the vintage clothing and well-known designer names such as Paul Smith and Michiko Koshino, the furnishings and fittings that you see are all for sale, too. The idea is that prices are reasonable, so there is a quick turnaround. The store setting changes frequently, and one is tempted to go back often because it always looks different. **Just north of map p. 52, 3A**

**High Tech** Piazza XXV Aprile 12. This is another store worth visiting, just for the experience, making the ideal link between Corso Garibaldi, which ends on one side of the piazza, and Corso Como, which starts on the other. High Tech is a furniture and furnishing emporium packed to the ceiling, a perfect place to find presents—not least for yourself. It's like a rabbit warren: you seem to go up the stairs to go down the stairs, doubling back on yourself and turning corners and running into dead-ends. The place is always busy and there are never enough assistants, but it's always fun. High Tech is open throughout the week, including Sundays. If you like the look and have half an afternoon to spare, take the shuttle bus to High Tech's warehouse store, called Cargo. The address is 39 Via Meucci, which is off Via Padova. **Just north of map p. 52, 3A**

# PORTA VENEZIA

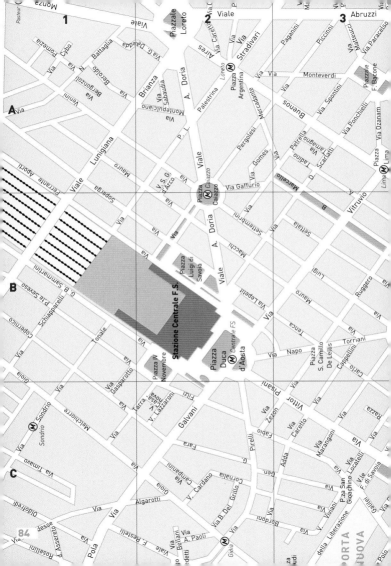

Porta Venezia, the east gate to the old city, once opened on a tree-lined avenue to Monza. Today the first stretch of that road, Corso Buenos Aires, is the main axis of the city's other major shopping district (after Via Montenapoleone), and the streets to the east and west host a multitude of contemporary art galleries. Milan's eastern and northeastern quarters, graced with lush, cool gardens, developed relatively late, and have some fine examples of early Modern architecture.

# Musei dei Giardini

## CIVICA GALLERIA D'ARTE MODERNA, PADIGLIONE D'ARTE CONTEMPORANEA AND MUSEO DEL CINEMA

The Public Gardens, which mark the northeast edge of the historic city centre, were created by Giuseppe Piermarini between 1783 and 1786. Originally designed in the formal Italian style, they were redesigned in the more 'natural' English style in 1862. Around this delightful green area are several fine museums.

**OPEN**    The Civica Galleria d'Arte Moderna is closed for renovation until late 2005 or early 2006; until then, guided visits of the space are held 9 am–11 am, Tue–Sun. The Padiglione d'Arte Contemporanea is open Tue–Sun, hours vary by exhibition The Museo del Cinema is open 3 pm–6 pm, Fri–Sun.

**CLOSED**    Civica Galleria d'Arte Moderna closed for renovation until late 2005 or early 2006. Padiglione d'Arte Contemporanea Mon, 1/1, 1/5, 25/12. Museo del Cinema Mon-Thur, 1/1, Easter Sunday, 25/4, 1/5, 1/7-15/9, 2/11, 8/12, 25-26/12

| CHARGES | Admission to the Civica Galleria d'Arte Moderna is free. Regular admission to the Padiglione d'Arte Contemporanea €6, reduced admission €3 Admission to the Museo del Cinema €3 |
|---|---|
| GUIDED VISITS | *Civica Galleria d'Arte Moderna* Tues-Sun 9 am and 11 am *Museo del Cinema* Guide available by appointment at 02 6698 6901 |
| DISABLED ACCESS | *Museo del Cinema* Wheelchair ramp |
| SERVICES | Café at the Padiglione d'Arte Contemporanea |
| TELEPHONE | *Civica Galleria d'Arte Moderna* 02 7600 2819 *Padiglione d'Arte Contemporanea* 02 7600 9085 *Museo del Cinema* 02 655 4977 |
| WEB | *Civica Galleria d'Arte Moderna* cimac-artecontemporeana.org *Padiglione d'Arte Contemporanea* www.pac-milano.org |
| MAIN ENTRANCE | *Civica Galleria d'Arte Moderna* Via Palestro 16 *Padiglione d'Arte Contemporanea* Via Palestro 14 *Museo del Cinema* Via Manin 2b |
| GETTING THERE | *Civica Galleria d'Arte Moderna, Padiglione d'Arte Contemporanea* M1 to Palestro *Museo del Cinema* M3 to Turati |

# CIVICA GALLERIA D'ARTE MODERNA
## HIGHLIGHTS
**Giuseppe Pellizza da Volpedo's *Quarto Stato***     First floor
**Francesco Hayez's *Portraits***

**Grassi bequest of French and Italian paintings**     Second floor

Across Via Palestro, along the south side of the Giardini Pubblici, is the Villa Belgiojoso, or Villa Reale. It was built for the influential Belgiojoso family in 1790 and later acquired by the sovereigns of Italy. It was once occupied by the Regent Eugène Beauharnais and by Field Marshal Radetzky, who died here in 1858. It has a sumptuous rear façade overlooking an attractive Romantic garden *all'inglese*, laid out in 1790 and now open as a public park. The villa is home to the Galleria d'Arte Moderna, which is undergoing renovation; tours covering some of the collection are available.

On the first floor, in the state rooms overlooking the garden, are

19th-C Lombard paintings, including the large *Quarto Stato*, a well-known work by **Giuseppe Pellizza da Volpedo** (another version of which hangs in the Brera, see p. 62). Other artists represented include **Antonio Canova**, and Italy's most celebrated Romantic painter, **Francesco Hayez**.

Stairs lead up to the second floor, where the large Carlo Grassi bequest of 19th-C French and Italian works is displayed.

The section dedicated to French painting includes works by Boudin, Sisley, Gauguin, Manet and van Gogh. In the last group of rooms are Italian paintings of the late 19th and early 20th centuries.

## PADIGLIONE D'ARTE CONTEMPORANEA

When the Villa Reale was chosen as the site for the Galleria d'Arte Moderna, it immediately became clear that the exhibition spaces were too small to accommodate larger works of contemporary art. A call went out for projects to renovate the former carriage house as a contemporary art pavilion, and the present design, by the architect Ignazio Gardella, was selected in 1948. The same architect renovated it in 1993 after it was damaged by a bomb (thought to be Mafia-related). Gardella's airy, flexible spaces are ideal for installations, with three distinct but connecting floors for sculpture, paintings and drawings, prints, photographs and large objects.

## MUSEO DEL CINEMA

The small but excellent Cinema Museum is located in the 17th-C Palazzo Dugnani (whose *Salone d'Onore* has frescoes by **Tiepolo**). It offers screenings of rare films and an eclectic collection, begun in 1947, that traces the history of motion pictures as far back as Galileo and his contemporaries. Alfred Hitchcock was one of the museum's most enthusiastic visitors (others have included Gina Lollobrigida, Frank Capra and Yul Brynner).

The most curious exhibits are in the section devoted to pre-cinema, which shows early attempts to project moving images. Historical instruments include an 18th-C Venetian invention called the *mondo novo*, which made it possible to view images on

*Mandala, Jukebox Speaker, Canti di Monaci Tibetani* (2002)
**Padiglione D'Arte Contemporanea**

perforated coloured prints by candlelight; 19th-C stereoscopes; and an 1867 zoetrope, which rotated a series of images on a cylinder to create an illusion of motion.

The photography section has daguerreotypes, a copy of **Eadweard Muybridge**'s *Human Figure in Motion* (1907), antique cameras and a portable photo laboratory.

The birth of motion pictures is shown with an original **Lumière** camera, made in Lyon in 1895, and early special effects are documented by the sketches and notebooks of Georges Méliès, inventor of the genre.

The silent film section has cameras, memorabilia, photographs by **Man Ray** and **Sergei Eisenstein**, and photograms from films by Germaine Dulac, René Clair and Luis Buñuel. Sound film is documented by a reconstruction of the set of **R. Mamoulian**'s *La Regina Cristina* with Greta Garbo (1933) and original sketches—notably by **Luchino Visconti** for *Senso* and **Federico Fellini** for *Le Notti di Cabiria*.

# in the area

**Museo di Storia Naturale & Planetario Hoepli** The most important natural history museum in Italy overlooks Corso Venezia from the shady grounds of the Giardini Pubblici. Its exhibits are extremely user-friendly. The Neoclassical Hoepli Planetarium stands on the same side of the gardens (entrance at Corso Venezia 57). Established in 1930, the planetarium is the largest in Italy, and the star shows beneath its 20-meter dome are not to be missed. **Map p. 85, 2B**

**Museo Treccani** (Via Carlo Porta 5; open 4 pm–7 pm, Wed and Thur; 02 657 2627). Ernesto Treccani was one of the founding members of the 20th-C Italian intellectual movement *Corrente*, which the Fascists found unpalatable and worked hard to suppress. In 1978, Treccani established a foundation to preserve his work (drawings, prints, sculpture and ceramics, as well as paintings) and to promote his aesthetic, a celebration of the working class and its struggle. **Map p. 85, 2C**

**Museo della Permanente** (Via Filippo Turati 34; open 10 am–1 pm and 2.30 pm–6.30 pm; admission €6.20; 02 6599 9803) This museum was designed as an exhibition space for cutting-edge art (the post-Impressionist Macchiaoli showed here in the 19th C, as did the Futurists in the 20th), but since 1999 it has hosted a small collection of works from the Civica Galleria d'Arte Moderna (see p. 86), which is closed for restoration. The first-floor exhibition space, renamed the Museum of the Twentieth Century (see p. 18) displays works by Boccioni, Modigliani, de Chirico and Fontana, among others. **Map p. 85, 1C**

**Piazza Cavour** The Piazza is notable for the Palazzo dei Giornali by Giovanni Muzio (1937–42), with external reliefs and an inside mosaic by Mario Sironiand. The piazza is named after Count Camillo Cavour, architect of Italian unification and King Vittorio Emanuele's first prime minister. There is a monument to him in the square. **Map p. 85, 2C**

# commercial galleries

**A Arte Studio Invernizzi** Via Scarlatti 12, 02 2940 2855, fax 02 2940 2855, www.aarteinvernizzi.it. The gallery represents European blue-chip artists: Gianni Asdrubali, Gianni Colombo, Dadamaino, François Morellet, Mario Nigro, Pino Pinelli, Bruno Querci, Nelio Sonego, Mauro Staccioli, Günter Umberg, Michel Verjux and Rudi Wach. **Map p. 84, 3A**

**Cannaviello** Via Stoppani 15, 02 2024 0428, fax 02 2040 4645, cannaviello@interfree.it. European cutting-edge contemporary art: Francesco De Grandi, Davide La Rocca, Bas Meerman, Federico Pietrella, Luigi Presicce, Pierluigi Pusole, Maja Vukoje. **Map p. 85, 2A**

**Istituto Grafico Italiano** Via Menotti 21, 02 2953 0058, fax 02 29522852, www.igi.mi.it. Prints by Italian artists such as Luca Alinari, Franz Borghese, Felice Bossone, Giuseppe Carì, Giorgio Cesati, Vittorio Maria Di Carlo, Ezio Farinelli, Giovan Francesco Gonzaga, Renato Guttuso, Francesco Messina, Antonio Perilli, Mario Schifano, Ernesto Treccani, Sandro Trotti. **Map p. 85, 3A**

**Lorenzelli** Corso Buenos Aires 2, 02 201914, fax 02 2940 1316, www.clubart.it/gallerie. European and American contemporary art by artists such as Natalino Andolfatto, Arcangelo, Giuliano Barbanti, Arturo Bonfanti, Luca Caccioni, Ronnie Cutrone, Herbert Ferber, Marco Gastini, Zoltan Kemeny, Osvaldo Licini, Zoran Music, Piero Pizzi Cannella, Luca Serra, Lee Ufan. **Map p. 85, 2B**

**Marconi** Via Tadino 15, 02 2940 4373, fax 02 2940 5573, www.giomarconi.com. Valerio Adami, Enrico Baj, Gianni Colombo, Lucio Del Pezzo, Bruno Di Bello, Chin Hsiao, Giuseppe Maraniello, Gianfranco Pardi, Arnoldo Pomodoro, Mimmo Rotella, Mario Schifano, Aldo Spoldi, Emilio Tadini, Joe Tilson, Giuseppe Uncini. **Map p. 85, 1B**

**Spiralearte** Corso Venezia 29, 02 795483, fax 02 795596. The gallery represents Sergi Barnils, Tommaso Cascella, Enzo Espositio, Marco Gastini, Giorgio Griffa, Franco Guerzoni, Joan Hernandez Pijuan, Medhat Shafik. **Map p. 85, 2B**

**Christian Stein** Corso Monforte 23, 02 7639 3301, fax 02 7600 7114, christianstein@iol.it. Italian and international contemporary art by top artists: Domenico Bianchi, Alighiero Boetti, Paolo Canevari, Luciano Fabro, Jannis Kounellis, Mario Merz, Marisa Merz, Mimmo Paladino, Giulio Paolini, Claudio Parmiggiani, Michelangelo Pistoletto, Remo Salvadori, Peter Wüthrich, Gilberto Zorio. **Map p. 85, 3B**

**Massimo De Carlo** Via Giovanni Ventura 5, 02 7000 3987/5, fax 02 7492135; Via Petrella 9, 02 20241550, www.massimodecarlo.it. Off the map. European cutting-edge contemporary artists: Mario Airò, Massimo Bartolini, Maurizio Cattelan, Roberto Cuoghi, Elmgreen & Dragset, Diego Perrone, Paola Pivi, Gregor Schneider, Ettore Spalletti, Rudolf Stingel, Piotr Uklanski.

# eat

## RESTAURANTS

€ **Da Giannino-L'Angolo d'Abruzzo** Via Pilo 20, corner of Via Nino Bixio, 02 2940 6526. A warm, friendly, place offering cooking from Abruzzo. **Map p. 85, 2A**

€€ **Al Girarrosto da Cesarina** Corso Venezia 31, 02 7600 0481. Restaurant specialising in Tuscan cuisine; closed Sat, Sunday lunchtime, all of Aug and Dec–Jan. **Map p. 85, 3C**

**Joia** Via Panfilo Castaldi 18, 02 2952 2124. Restaurant known for its fine vegetarian cuisine. Prepare to be surprised; the Italian take on vegetarian may be different, and more delicious, than what you expect. Closed Sat lunchtimes, Sundays, Easter, Aug and Dec–Jan. **Map p. 85, 1B**

**L'Osteria del Treno** Via San Gregorio 46–48, 02 670 0479. Originally an after-work place for railway workers (hence the name), this restaurant has become very fashionable in recent years. If you have heard of the slow food movement and want to know more, this is the place to come. Closed Sat, Sunday lunchtimes and two weeks in Aug, as well as Christmas to New Year's Day. **Map p. 84, 3C**

€€€**Calajunco** Via Ramazzini 4, 02 2951 2263. Restaurant specialising in Sicilian cuisine from the Aeolian Islands. Closed lunchtimes, Sundays, Aug and from Christmas to Jan 6. **Map p. 85, 2A**

## A MILANO EXPERIENCE

**Pizzeria Spontini** Via Spontini, corner of Corso Buenos Aires, 02 204 7444, www.pizzeriaspontini.it. This is the Italian version of a greasy spoon: first you line up behind everyone else, then you sit at a formica-topped table with paper tablemat and napkin. Pizza is ordered by the slice (*al trancio*), either normal or with extra cheese. You can also order water, beer, and coffee. That's it. The pizzeria is closed Mondays, the whole of August, and between Christmas and Jan 6. **Map p. 84, 3A**

For dessert, stop by a local gelateria, such as **Viel** (Corso Buenos Aires 15), where the range of sorbet is unparalleled. **Map p. 85, 1C**

## WINE BARS

**Ombre Rosse** Via Plinio 29, 02 29524734. This wine bar is good for light food like salamis, cheeses and salads. Then drink a glass of *passito* with your sweet. There are over three hundred wines in the cellar. Open 6.30 pm–1 am, closed Sundays and Aug. **Map p. 85, 1A**

## HAPPY HOUR

**Diana Garden** Hotel Sheraton Diana Majestic, Piazza Oberdan, at Viale Piave, 02 2058 2081 or 02 6230 4029. Although other places in Milan offer 'happy hour' drinks and snacks, usually between 6.30 pm and 9 pm, the garden of the Hotel Diana is still a special experience. It's all to do with décor, which of course changes every year—the latest style being sofas, leather armchairs, and chandeliers. Drinks in the garden of this 5-star hotel cost about €10. **Map p. 85, 2B**

## CAFÉS

€ **Bell'Aurore** Via Castelmorrone, on the corner with Via Abamonti. This is probably Milan's only café on the French model. Have a coffee here, or even lunch. There are tables outside during the spring and summer. **Map p. 85, 2A**

# shop

## CLOTHING

What Via Montenapoleone is to the city centre and the Brera district of Milan, Corso Buenos Aires is to Porta Venezia. Running from Porta Venezia metro stop (**Map p. 85, 2B**) via the Lima metro stop to Piazzale Loreto (**Map p. 84, 2A**) and intersected by crosstown buses 60, 90, 91 and 92, as well as the 33 tram, Corso Buenos Aires is every inch a shopping street. That's a lot of inches and a lot of shops, so be sure to plan accordingly if you want to shop here. Note that Saturdays are especially hectic, when people from the province come in to shop. There are no top designer names, but there are some great chain stores: **Benetton**, **JDC (Jeanseria de Corso)**, **Liu-Jo**, **Luisa Spagnoli**, **Marina Rinaldi**, **Nadine**, **Phard**, **ProMod**, **Sem**, **Sisley** and **Zara**. For handbags, try **Furla**, **Coccinelle**, and **Mandarina Duck**. For department stores, there's a **UPIM** near the corner of the Corso with Viale Tunisia and another at Piazzale Loreto. Next door, you'll find is a **COIN**.

## FOOTWEAR

For shoes, there's **Kammi** and **Vergelio** on Corso Buenos Aires. If you have large feet, most Italian shoe stores cannot help. But try Ghigodonna at Viale Tunisia 2, on the corner of Corso Buenos Aires (**Map p. 85, 1B**), which carries shoes through to a size 46.

## OUTLETS

**Salvagente** Via Fratelli Bronzetti 16, on the corner of Via Archimede. In addition to top name men's and women's designer gear, from Prada to Armani to Alberta Ferretti, there's also well-priced boutique clothes, including great sweaters, trousers and skirts, at this hard-to-find outlet. The end-of-season sales, at the end of Dec and early July, offer especially good value: they start at 30% off and end at 50%–70% off in the last ten days. To get there, take the 60 bus and get off at the stop nearest the corner with Via Archimede. Find the green gate, next to the hairdressers. Go down the driveway. Note that they take cash only (there's an ATM at the bank on the corner of Via Archimede). Shop hours are 10 am–12.30 pm and 3 pm–7 pm on Tue–Fri; closed Mon morning; and 10 am–7pm, Wed and Sat.

**Affari** Corner of Via Marcona and Via Bronzetti. If you are a fan of Midali (see p. 81) then stop here. It's just 200 m from Salvagente, so it's worth combining the two in one trip. **Just south of map p. 85, 3A**

# ANTIQUES

The whole block of Via Carlo Pisacane between Piazza VIII Novembre and Via Nino Bixio (**Map p. 85, 2A**) is full of antique shops, including **Il Quadrifoglio Via Pisacane**, **Antichità Giglio & C.**, **Antichità Porta Venezia** and **Piave Antichità** .

At Christmas, all the antique stores in Via Pisacane organise a joint exhibition. If you have time, walk the length of the street, right the way down to Corso Indipendenza. On the way, you will be able to admire many fine examples of the Milan version of the Italian take on Art Nouveau (called Liberty in Italian). At Corso Indipendenza, you can pick up the 54 or 61 bus to get back into the centre of town. Or walk to Piazzale Dateo where you can take the *passante*, or blue line. The first stop is Corso Venezia on the red line. On the way to the passante station, check out **Il Valore Aggiunto** at Via Mameli, 3.

# THE HOME

**Al mercatino tra noi e voi** Via Marcora 8. Ring the bell marked *mercatino* and you will be buzzed into this basement treasure trove of second-hand furniture, lighting and household goods. Open 10.30 am–12.30 pm and 3 pm–7.30 pm. Closed Tue. **Map p. 85, 1C**

**Avant de Dormir** Via Turati 3, just by Piazza Cavour. An eclectic place where you can find all sorts of interesting stuff for the home, for presents, or just to look at, picked out with loving fondness by the owners. **Map p. 85, 2C**

**Frette** Corso Buenos Aires, corner Via Pecchio. Top-of-the-line household linens in lovely colours and textures, and a reminder that some people do still use sheets, blankets and bedspreads. Exquisite embroidery for the trousseau, but remember that the Italians still consider ironing an essential part of the domestic routine. **Map p. 84, 2A**

**Kartell** Corner of Via Turati and Via Carlo Porta. The huge, curved plate-glass windows of this corner store mean that the entire shop is the window display. Gaze in wonder at what Philippe Starck, Ron Arad, Patricia Urquiola, Antonio Citterio, Alberto Meda and Vico Magistretti, among others, manage to do with plastic and Perspex. **Map p. 85, 2C**

**Spotti** Viale Piave 27. If you fancy some window shopping for furniture, this is a good place to start. The vast plate glass windows allow you to room sets by companies like Agape, Alias, Arc Linea, B&B Italia, Cappellini, Driade, Flexform, Knoll, Maxalto, Porro and Vitra. **Map p. 85, 2B**

## BOOKS

**Borsa de Fumetto** Via Lecco 16. The Italians are not great readers: just 42% of the over-15 age group says they read regularly, says Italy's publishers' association, compared to an EU average of 45% and a UK average of 63%. On the other hand, they love their comic books, and if you are a fan, you are likely to find a lot to keep you amused. **Map p. 85, 1B**

**L'Atlante di Paolo Vitolo** Via Tadino 30. Rare and out-of-print books on modern and contemporary culture, especially the avant-garde movements in art, literature, music, architecture, cinema and theatre. **Map p. 85, 3B**

**Libreria dell'Automobile** Corso Venezia 43. The Italians have designed some great looking cars. They also go for great-looking coffee table books. This store combines the two, and is the place to go if you are looking for a colourful book on your favourite car. **Map p. 85, 3C**

## CHILDREN

**Prenatal** Corso Buenos Aires 26. Just about everything for young children, babies and mums-to-be, from clothes to prams to toys, games and books. Even if you are addicted to Mothercare, check it out. There are lots of stores around town: including Corso Vittorio Emanuele II 13, Corso XXII Marzo 4, Corso Vercelli 51, corner of Via Cimarosa, Via Dante 7. **Map p. 85, 1B**

**Salvagente Bimbi** Via Balzaretti 28. Off the map. The kids' version of the Salvagente designer outlet is a short walk from the Piola metro station, on the green line.

# SANT'AMBROGIO

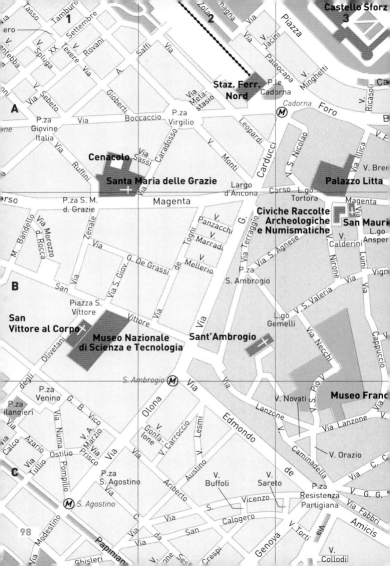

This area, due west of the Duomo, is probably the most expensive residential neighbourhood in Italy. The stately old flats, many in period-revival buildings, overlook shady boulevards and wide, elegant streets. It is also home to one of Milan's most beautiful churches—Sant'Ambrogio.

# Sant'Ambrogio

| | |
|---|---|
| **OPEN** | The church is open every day, 8 am–12 pm and 2.30 pm–6 pm. The Museo di Sant'Ambrogio is open every day, 10 am–12 pm and 3 pm–5 pm. |
| **CLOSED** | *Museo di Sant'Ambrogio* In June-Sept, on Mon; in Oct-May, on Tues; and 1/1, Easter Day, 25/4, 1/5, all of August. |
| **CHARGES** | No charge for the church; regular admission to the Museo di Sant'Ambrogio €3.00 |
| **GUIDED VISITS** | By reservation, 02 8645 0895 |
| **DISABLED ACCESS** | Yes |
| **TELEPHONE** | *Museo di Sant'Ambrogio* 02 8645 0895 |
| **MAIN ENTRANCE** | Piazza Sant'Ambrogio 15 |
| **GETTING THERE** | M2 to Sant'Ambrogio |

## HIGHLIGHTS

| | |
|---|---|
| **Lombard Romanesque architecture and decoration** | Exterior and interior |
| **Romanesque pulpit and Roman palaeo-Christian sarcophagus** | Nave |
| **9th-C mosaics** | Sacello di San Vittore in Ciel d'Oro |
| **9th-C ciborium**<br>**High altar with jewel-encrusted 9th-C gold and silver casing** | Sanctuary |

Sant'Ambrogio, the most interesting church in Milan, is one of the most characteristic examples of Lombard Romanesque architecture. Founded by St Ambrose, Bishop of Milan, it was built in 379–86 beside a Christian cemetery, then enlarged in the 9th and 11th centuries. The present building is the result of numerous careful restorations—a radical restoration in the 19th C was followed by serious war damage in 1943—and the dating of the various parts of the building is still uncertain.

## EXTERIOR

The splendid atrium in front of the church, on an early Christian plan, was probably built in 1088–99 and was reconstructed in 1150. The austere façade consists of a five-bayed porch below and five arches above, graduated to fit the slope of the gable. The south, or monks', campanile dates from the 9th C, while the higher, so-called canons' campanile on the north is a fine Lombard tower of 1128–44, crowned with a loggia of 1889. The great doorway has wood imposts made up of fragments from the 8th and 10th centuries (heavily restored in the 18th C) and the bronze doors date from the 11th–12th C.

## INTERIOR

The beautiful interior has a low rib-vaulted nave divided from the side aisles by wide arcades. The arcades supported by massive pillars beneath a women's gallery. There are no transepts, and beyond the tower over the crossing are three deep apses, the centre one raised above the crypt. On the left, beyond a column with a 10th-C bronze serpent, is the **pulpit**, one of the most remarkable Romanesque monuments known. It was reconstituted from gorgeous 11th- and 12th-C fragments saved after the vault collapsed in 1196.

**SOUTH AISLE** The first chapel on the on the south side of the church has a fresco attributed to **Gaudenzio Ferrari** and **Giovanni Battista della Cerva**. The second chapel has an altarpiece by

The atrium of Sant'Ambrogio

Ferrari and two detached frescoes by **Tiepolo**. At the end is the **Sacello di San Vittore in Ciel d'Oro**, a sepulchral chapel built in a Christian cemetery in the 4th C and altered later. Its name refers to the splendid 5th-C mosaics, with six panels representing saints (including St Ambrose) on the walls. The capitolino, between the sacello and the Benedictine monastery, holds exhibits from the Museo di Sant'Ambrogio.

**NORTH AISLE** The first chapel has a fresco of the *Redeemer* by **Bergognone**, and, in the third chapel, a tondo attributed to **Bernardino Luini**.

**SANCTUARY** Under the dome (which was rebuilt in the 13th C and restored in the 19th C) is the great **ciborium**, thought to date from the 9th C. The shafts of the columns, however, are probably of the time of St Ambrose. The four sides of the canopy are decorated with reliefs in coloured stucco in the Byzantine style (mid-10th C).

The **altar** has a magnificent casing presented to the church in 835. It is made of gold and silver plates sculptured in relief with enamel and gems and representing scenes from the lives of Christ and St Ambrose. In the apse are 4th- or 8th-C mosaics (reset in the 18th C and restored again after World War II) and the 9th-C marble bishop's throne.

The crypt contains the body of St Ambrose and two others, referred to as the bodies of the early martyrs Gervase and Protasius. Ambrose, when he was Bishop of Milan, had the whereabouts of the bodies revealed to him in a dream and brought them to his new and splendid basilica, where they still rest.

**PORTICO DELLA CANONICA** From the east end of the north aisle a door leads to the Portico della Canonica with columns carved in imitation of tree trunks. The portico was left unfinished by **Bramante** in 1499 and reconstructed after World War II, and a second side was added in 1955. The upper part now houses the **Museo di Sant'Ambrogio**. The collections include the robe of St Ambrose (protected by a curtain); early Christian mosaic fragments; 4th-C wood fragments from the old doors of the

basilica; frescoes by **Bergognone** and **Bernardino Luini**; and two 17th-C Flemish tapestries, depicting the *Triumph of Constantine*, on designs by **Peter Paul Rubens**.

To the north of the church is a **war memorial** erected in 1928 by Giovanni Muzio. The distinguished Università Cattolica, founded in 1921, fronts the piazza here. It is housed in the former monastery of Sant'Ambrogio, which includes two fine cloisters designed by Bramante. Roman remains have come to light here during work to enlarge the buildings.

# Museo Nazionale di Scienza e Tecnologia

| | |
|---|---|
| **OPEN** | The museum is open 9.30 am–5 pm, Tues–Fri, and 9.30 am–6.30 pm, Sat–Sun and holidays. |
| **CLOSED** | Mon, 1/1, 25/12 |
| **CHARGES** | Regular admission €7; under 18 years or over 60 €5 |
| **DISABLED ACCESS** | Yes (ask at Reception) |
| **SERVICES** | Bookshop, café/restaurant |
| **TELEPHONE** | 02 485 551 |
| **WEB** | www.museoscienza.org |
| **MAIN ENTRANCE** | Via San Vittore 21 |
| **GETTING THERE** | M2 to Sant'Ambrogio |

This former Olivetan convent (1507) was rebuilt in 1949–53 after war damage to house the huge **Museo Nazionale di Scienza e Tecnica Leonardo da Vinci** . With its twenty-eight sections, covering everything from information technology to train engines to astronomy, this is one of the most important technical and scientific museums in the world.

## COLLECTION

The museum highlights a special moment in Italy's artistic history: the birth of the 'Renaissance man', epitomised by **Leonardo da Vinci**. Leonardo was famous for his ability to unite art, science and technology—fields that have become increasingly divided over the centuries—and a large gallery is dedicated to his genius as engineer and scientist, with models of his machines displayed alongside frescoes from the 14th to the 18th C. Among these is a reproduction of Leonardo's *Last Supper*, the original of which can be found at Santa Maria delle Grazie, only 200 metres from the museum (see p. 108).

The *first floor* display take you on a tour through the **history of crafts**. On the right is the Sala della Bifora (usually kept locked), with the Mauro collection of **gold and precious stones**, flanked by a reconstructed goldsmith's shop with tools and equipment for melting, laminating, sculpting and etching. The gallery is devoted to **photography and cinematography**, from the 16th-C camera obscura to the first real photograph (1826) and the **Lumière** brothers' first moving picture (1895). Rooms to the right demonstrate the evolution of the graphic arts up till and including the time of printing.

At the end of the gallery, to the right, is the long *Leonardo Gallery*, which extends the entire length of the first and second cloisters. The **machines** exhibited here are all based on the artist/inventor's drawings, which are displayed together with modern diagrams and descriptions of how the inventions work. There are more than a hundred static models and seven working models: an aerial screw, revolving crane, Archimedes' screw, pulley system, weight-lifting machine, device for testing beating wings, and a flying machine with manoeuvrable wing-tips.

Multimedia aids add to the experience by exploring questions such as whether these machines could have worked. Although the answer is often 'no', credit is nonetheless due to the great artist for many brilliant ideas that would be successfully implemented in subsequent centuries.

The rooms (right) that border the first cloister are devoted to **time and sound**, including musical instruments. Three galleries round the second cloister illustrate **physics**, including electricity, acoustics and nuclear physics. Beyond the astronomy gallery are rooms devoted to **optics** and to **radio and telecommunications**.

The *lower floor* exhibit is devoted to metallurgy, the petrochemical industries and **transport**, with a fine gallery of early motor cars. Outside are the external pavilions:

The *Padiglione Ferroviario (Rail Transport Building)*, in the form of a 19th-C railway station, contains railway locomotives and rolling stock.

The huge *Edificio Aeronavale (Air & Sea Transport Building)* has a splendid display of airplanes and exhibits on nautical and aeronautical history.

The *Giardini della Scienza* (a hands-on 'gardens of science') is a green, leafy park with interactive scientific displays.

### Leonardo's manuscripts

Leonardo's restless and brilliant mind led him through many areas of study, including engineering, painting and architecture (he often left projects half-finished, stimulated by the thought of something new). After Leonardo's death (in Paris in 1519), his pupil Francesco Melzi returned to Italy carrying many of the master's manuscripts and drawings, full of sketches and designs.

Melzi was careful to preserve them as Leonardo had left them, but his heirs were less meticulous. Some of the drawings were lost, others were given away or sold, others still taken as war booty (by Napoleon, for example, in 1796). The notebooks originally presented the train of Leonardo's eclectic thoughts as they occured to him, but at some point they were torn up and pieced back together by theme.

Today the known, extant drawings of Leonardo are divided into ten different manuscripts: the *Codex Arundel* (British Library, London); the *Codex Atlanticus* (Biblioteca Ambrosiana, Milan); the *Codex Trivulzianus* (Biblioteca Trivulziana, Castello Sforzesco, Milan); the *Codex on the Flight of Birds* (Biblioteca Reale, Turin); the *Codex Ashburnham* and *Codices of the Institut de France* (Institut de France, Paris); the *Codex Forste* (Victoria and Albert Museum, London); the *Codex Leicester* (purchased by Bill Gates in 1995); the *Windsor Folios* (Royal Collection, Windsor Castle); and the *Madrid Codices* (National Library, Madrid). The set in Madrid was only discovered in 1966, quite by accident; much of Leonardo's output is still missing.

# Santa Maria delle Grazie and the Cenacolo

| | |
|---|---|
| **OPEN** | The Cenacolo is open 8.15 am–6.45 pm. Reservations are required (see below). |
| **CLOSED** | Mon, 1/1 |
| **CHARGES** | Regular admission €6.20, reduced €3.10; free for European Union citizens under 18 or over 60 |
| **GUIDED VISITS** | Audio guides; English-language guide available on request at 02 8942 1146 |
| **DISABLED ACCESS** | Yes (ask at Reception) |
| **TELEPHONE** | Cenacolo Information and reservations 02 8942 1146; reservations only 02 498 7588 |
| **MAIN ENTRANCE** | Cenacolo Information and reservations 02 8942 1146; reservations only 02 498 7588 |
| **GETTING THERE** | M1 to Conciliazione |

## HIGHLIGHTS

| | |
|---|---|
| **Leonardo da Vinci's *Last Supper*** | Cenacolo |
| **Bramante's crossing and small cloister** | Church |

A church of brick and terracotta with a very beautiful exterior, Santa Maria delle Grazie was erected in 1466–90 to a design by Guiniforte Solari. In 1492 Lodovico il Moro ordered the striking new choir and unusual domed crossing. The latter has long been attributed to Bramante, although it is now uncertain how much he was directly involved. The fine west portal is also often attributed to Bramante.

## INTERIOR

Inside, the nave vault and aisles have fine frescoed decorations of c. 1482–85 (restored in 1937). In the aisles, between the chapels, are frescoes of Dominican saints. The first chapel in the south aisle has a fine tomb of the Della Torre family; in the third chapel are lunette frescoes attributed to Aurelio and Gian Piero Luini. The fourth chapel has frescoes by **Gaudenzio Ferrari** (1542), and in the fifth are stucco bas-reliefs (late 16th-C) of angels.

The lovely light tribuna, or domed crossing, believed to have been designed by **Bramante**, has unusual bright *graffiti* decoration. The choir also has *graffiti* and fine stalls of carved and inlaid wood. A door leads out to the small cloister (*chiostrino*), also traditionally attributed to Bramante, with its pretty little garden.

At the end of the north aisle is the elaborate entrance to the

**Santa Maria delle Grazie**

chapel of the Madonna delle Grazie, which has a highly venerated 15th-C painting of the *Madonna* beneath a vault with restored 15th-C frescoes. The sixth chapel has a small *Holy Family* by **Paris Bordone**, and the second chapel has a funerary monument with sculptures attributed to **Bambaia**. The first chapel has frescoes by Giovanni Donato Montorfano.

## CENACOLO

In the cenacolo, or refectory,of the adjoining Dominican convent is the famous *Last Supper* by **Leonardo da Vinci**, painted in 1494–97. In order to protect the painting from dust and lessen the effects of pollution, visitors (in groups of only 15 or 20 at a time) go through a series of glass cubicles with air-filtering systems.

This extraordinary painting, which was to have a lasting effect on generations of painters, depicts the moment when Christ announces Judas's betrayal at the Last Supper. The monumental figures of the Apostles are shown in an extension of the refectory itself, in perfect perspective. The light enters both through the real windows on the left and the painted windows in the background, which look out over a landscape, and the wonderful colours culminate in the blue and red robe of Christ. Note the Apostles' robes reflected in the pewter plates and the transparent glass carafes. Above are lunettes with garlands of fruit and flowers around the coats of arms of the Sforza family. On the side walls Leonardo painted tapestries decorated with bunches of flowers. There is no evidence that Leonardo made use of a cartoon while working on this masterpiece.

### *Leonardo's technique*

The *Last Supper* is painted with a technique peculiar to Leonardo, in tempera with the addition of later oil varnishes on a prepared surface, in two layers on the plastered wall. It is therefore not a fresco, and errors in the preparation of the plaster, together with the dampness of the wall, have caused great damage to the painted surface. This had already considerably deteriorated by the beginning of the 16th C. Since that time it has been restored repeatedly, and was twice repainted (in oils) in the 18th C. Careful work (begun in 1978 and completed in 1999) has been carried out to eliminate the false restorations of the past and to expose the original work of Leonardo as far as possible. The restoration, like that of Michelangelo's Sistine Ceiling in Rome, has sparked considerable controversy.

On the wall opposite the *Last Supper* is a large *Crucifixion* by Donato Montorfano (1495), the fine state of which shows the lasting quality of true fresco painting. The fresco decoration on the long wall is attributed to Bernardino de' Rossi. At the bottom of the fresco, at either side, are kneeling figures (now nearly effaced) added by Leonardo before 1498 (showing Lodovico il Moro and his wife Beatrice d'Este and their two children).

# Civiche Raccolte Archeologiche e Numismatiche

| | |
|---|---|
| **OPEN** | The museum is open 9 am–5.30 pm, Tue–Sun. |
| **CLOSED** | Mon, 1/1, 1/5, 25/12 |
| **CHARGES** | Free |
| **GUIDED VISITS** | Audio tours available; guided tours by Società Cooperativa Archeologica 02 867 336 |
| **DISABLED ACCESS** | Yes (ask at Reception) |
| **TELEPHONE** | 02 8645 0011, 02 8846 5720 |
| **MAIN ENTRANCE** | Corso Magenta 15 |
| **METRO** | M1 to Cordusio/Cadorna, M2 to Cadorna |

## HIGHLIGHTS
**Coppa Trivulzio**
**Parabiago Patera**

Ground floor

The main collections of the Municipal Museum of Antiquities, with Greek, Etruscan and Roman material relating to the history of Milan, occupy the monumental Monastero Maggiore di San Maurizio. It is planned to move the collections (together with the Egyptian and prehistorical collections, now at the Castello Sforzesco, p. 63) to more spacious quarters in the former Ansaldo Steel Works, but for the time being they are beautifully displayed in this impressive historic setting.

## CLOISTERS
In the cloisters are Roman sculpture and a large incised stone from Valle Camonica dating from the late Bronze Age.

## GROUND FLOOR

The highlight of the ground floor exhibits is the famous *Coppa Trivulzio*, a double coloured glass drinking cup of intricate workmanship with the inscription 'Drink and live many years', dating from the early 4th C AD. It was found in a sarcophagus near Novara in 1675.

The silver *Parabiago Patera*, with Attis and Cybele and other fine figures in relief, is a Roman work of the late 4th C AD. Other exhibits include a fine collection of antique vases, Roman sculpture (including a colossal torso of Hercules), mosaics and other finds. There is also a section devoted to barbarian invaders of Lombardy, with Gothic, Germanic and Lombard gold, arms and armour.

## LOWER LEVEL

In the basement are Etruscan material and Indian Gandhara sculpture (2nd–3rd-C AD). The hall beyond has a chronological and topographical display of Greek ceramics, including Attic red- and black-figure vases. At the end of the room you can see the base of a stretch of Roman wall, once part of the city walls.

In the **GARDEN** is the Torre di Ansperto, an octagonal tower of Roman origin, with interesting traces of 13th-C frescoes and a Roman sarcophagus of the 3rd C AD.

# in the area

**Palazzo Clerici** Beyond Piazza Cordusio, on Via Clerici, is Palazzo Clerici, in the hall of which is a magnificent ceiling painting by Tiepolo (1740). **Map p. 99, 2B**

**San Vittore al Corpo** Built in part by Galeazzo Alessi, it contains important early 17th-C works, including frescoes and paintings by Camillo

**Palazzo Clerici**

Procaccini. The cupola is frescoed by Moncalvo and Daniele Crespi and the beautifully carved choir stalls date from around 1583. In the north aisle are frescoes and paintings by Daniele Crespi and an altarpiece by Pompeo Batoni. **Map p. 98, 1B**

**San Maurizio** The church adjoining the Archaeological Museum was begun in 1503, though the façade dates from around1574–81. The harmonious interior is divided by a wall into two parts. The western portion, originally for lay worshippers, has small chapels below and a graceful loggia above, and contains numerous frescoes by Bernardino Luini and his sons and other members of his school. In the loggia are frescoed medallions by Boltraffio (1505–10). **Map p.98, 3B**

**Palazzo Borromeo** In an office (admission on request) off the second courtyard of this reconstructed 15th-C building are interesting frescoes depicting card games and other pursuits by a painter of the early 15th C, done in the International Gothic style. **Map p. 98, 1B**

**Business district** Centered on Piazza Edison and Piazza degli Affari is the main business district of Milan, with the Stock Exchange and a number of banks, most of them built at the beginning of the 20th century. Piazza Cordusio was laid out in 1889–1901 as the financial centre of the city. **Map p. 99, 2A**

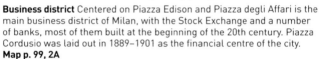

# commercial galleries

**La Spirale 2000** Via Marradi 1, 02 805 6685 or 878 827, fax 02 8645 4241, www.laspirale2000.com. Ottavio Missoni, Massimo Campigli, Giorgio De Chrico, Marino Marini, Ugo Nespolo, Pablo Picasso, Giampaolo Talani. **Map p. 98, 2B**

**Le Case d'Arte** Via Gorani 8, 02 805 4071. International contemporary art, especially by younger artists. **Map p. 99, 1B**

**Tonelli** Corso Magenta 85, 02 481 2434, fax 02 481 2434, www.galleriatonelli.com. Matthias Brandes, Giorgio De Chirico, Filippo De Pisis, Piero Dorazio, Lucio Fontana, Giorgio Morandi, Mario Sironi, Tancredi, Emilio Vedova. **Map p. 98, 1A**

# eat

## RESTAURANTS

**€€ Cantina della Vetra** Via Papa Pio IV 3, corner of Piazza della Vetra, 02 8940 3843. Some may call it a wine bar—and the fact that owner Herbert Messinese makes available a different list of one hundred bottles each week confirms that the wine-lover is well served here—but unlike the average Italian wine bar, which for food sticks to cold cuts and cheese, this place has a full menu. Try the *burrata*, a speciality of the Puglia area of southern Italy, a large mozzarella filled with fresh cream. Risotto with lemon and herbs is also exceptional. The location is right behind the basilica di San Lorenzo, one of Milan's most beautiful churches. **Map p. 99, 1C**

**Uccellina** Corso Magenta 96, corner of Piazza Baracca, 02 4800 0728. This place is what is referred to, in Italian, as a *pizzeria con cucina,* which means pizza isn't the only dish on offer. The name refers to the Parco dell'Uccellina in Tuscany, and this is the theme of the décor as well as the food. On the pizza side, the house speciality is Tuscan sausage and porcini mushrooms, as well as the focaccia with *lardo di Colonnata.* If you want to try something from the cucina, opt for *pappardelle al cinghiale*, *ribollita* or grilled meat or fish. Reservations advised, as it is known for staying open when other restaurants are closed. Closed Christmas and New Year's Day. Open in Aug. **Map p. 98, 1B**

**€€€Orti di Leonardo** Via Aristide De Togni 6/8, 02 498 3476. The Leonardo in question is da Vinci himself, who was given land in this neighbourhood while he was working across the street at the church of Santa Maria delle Grazie (see p. 108). The *orti* were the kitchen gardens of Leonardo's residence. Set in Palazzo delle Stelline, which is now a conference centre, this spacious restaurant specialises in creative interpretations of Italian dishes and Continental cuisine. Closed Sundays, all of Aug, Christmas to Jan 6. **Map p. 98, 2B**

### OUT OF THE WAY BUT WORTH IT

**€€€Il Luogo di Aimo e Nadia** Via Montecuccoli 6, 02 416 886, www.aimoenadia.com. This Michelin one-star is widely considered to be Milan's finest restaurant, and the long cab ride from the centre of town is worth it for the restaurant's traditional and innovative cuisine. Closed Sat lunchtime and Sundays; three weeks in Aug; Jan 1–10.

## CAFÉS

**€**   **San Carlo** Via Bandello 1. This street is the first right on Corso Magenta as you come from Piazza Baracca on your way to Santa Maria delle Grazie. It is a great place for cappuccino and brioche at breakfast, or stop here for a light lunch of a *panino* and a drink. **Map p. 98, 1B**

**€€**   **Marchesi** Corso Magenta 13, on the corner of Via Santa Maria alla Porta and Via Meravigli. The outside has delicate *sgraffito*; the inside of this small *pasticceria-caffetteria* has cakes on sale on one side and the bar on the other. For panettone fans, you can get this traditional Christmas cake year round. Closed Sun afternoon and all day Mon, as is the case with many shops that sell fresh cakes and pastries. Also closed Aug. **Map p. 98, 3B**

# shopping

The main shopping street in this neck of the woods is Corso Vercelli (**Map p. 98, 3B**), the continuation of Corso Magenta (map p. 98, 1–2B). The stores are all pretty upmarket, reflecting the area, and even the **COIN** department store seems smarter than some of the other branches in other parts of town. Among the chain stores you will find in Corso Vercelli are **Benetton**, **Lacoste**, **L'altra moda**, **Luisa Spagnoli**, **Marlboro Classic**, **Max&Co**, **Puma**, **Sisley** and **Stefanel**.

There is a lovely little concentration of smaller shops with some exquisite merchandise where Via Meravigli ends, near the Marchesi pasticceria (see above). To the left is Via Santa Maria della Porta, where you will find the Milan outpost of the **Officina Profumeria di Santa Maria Novella**. To the left is Via San Giovanni alle Mura, with exquisite window displays in the shops of the local jewellers.

## ACCESSORIES

**DEV** Corso Vercelli 8. DEV stands for Della Valle, and this store carries the company's top brands: Tod's, Hogan and Fay shoes and bags. For apparel, seek out the individual boutiques in the city centre. **Just west of map p. 98, 1A**

**Furla** Corso Vercelli 11, corner of Largo Settimio Severo. One of the more exciting mid-range Italian handbag manufacturers. Check out the costume jewellery and watches, too. Also Corso Vittorio Emanuele, on the corner of Via San Paolo and Furla corner in the Rinascente department store, Corso Vittorio Emanuele, Corso Buenos Aires, on the corner of Via Omboni. If you're at the airport and you decide on a last-minute purchase, then head for the Furla store in Terminal 1. **Just west of map p. 98, 1A**

**Louise Lanzi** Via Santa Maria Fulcorina 20. Louise Lanzi is an American jeweller based in Milan. She is known for a rich, simple look that puts beautifully coloured gemstones into prominence. Call for an appointment. **Map 98, 1B**

**Mandarina Duck** Corso Vercelli 27. Trendy high-tech travel bags and cases, plus men's and women's sportswear, watches and other accessories. Also at Corso Europa, on the corner of Galleria San Carlo. **Just west of map p. 98, 1A**

## ANTIQUES

Milan's best event for antiques is held here in and around the Piazza Sant'Ambrogio (Map p.98, 2B) and environs during the week of Dec 7, the feast day of St Ambrose.

The street fair is called 'Bej, o bej', which in Milanese dialect is an expression of delight at beauty. Piazza Sant'Ambrogio is given over to stalls selling knick-knacks, and antique dealers set up stands in the streets for this crowded and visited season.

**Era l'Ora** Corso Magenta 22. The Italians are great collectors of timepieces, and this shop carries vintage Patek Philippe, Rolex and Vacheron&Costantin, among others. Also pocket watches, wall clocks, grandfather clocks. **Map p. 98, 3B**

**Hutong Gallery** Via Lanzone 5. Specialising in Asian art, this gallery has terracotta statues, rare Chinese furniture, lacquered boxes and jewellery. Also carpets from China and Tibet. **Map p. 98, 3C**

**Il Bulino** Corso Magenta 50. Original prints by old and modern masters. **Map p. 98, 2B**

**L'Oggetto Ritrovato Gallery** Corso Magenta 14. Step through into the courtyard to visit this gallery, which specialises in 20th-C glass and furniture. **Map p. 98, 3B**

**Michail di David Sorgato** Via Sant'Orsola 13. This is the place for those who love old and antique textiles. David Sorgato has searched the world for beautiful rugs and wall hangings. **Map p. 98, 3B**

**Vecchi Monili – Antiquariato Navale** Via Caminadella 18. Milan is at least three hours from the sea, but nonetheless this antique store specialises in naval instruments, furniture and paintings. Also globes, maps and charts. **Map p. 98, 3C**

## THE HOME

**Area Design** Via Borromei 11. Furniture and lighting from 1960s to the 1980s, by the best Italian designers, including Joe Colombo, Achille Castiglioni, Ettore Sottsass and Marco Zanuso. **Map p. 99, 1B**

**Frette** Corso Vercelli 23-25. Top-of-the-line household linens in lovely colours and textures. Also at Corso Buenos Aries, corner Via Pecchio, Via Torino 42, Via Manzoni 11. **Just west of map p. 98, 1A**

**Sag '80** Via Boccaccio 4, 02 4815380/02, fax 498 7393. Furniture for home and office, from the likes of B&B Italia, Boffi, Cassina, Dada, Flou, Frau, Giorgetti, Knoll, Minotti, Molteni, Porro and Zanotta. **Map p. 98, 2A**

## CHILDREN

**BabyMotta** Corso Vercelli 6, corner of Largo Settimio Severo. If you want to see what the well-dressed Italian baby is wearing, and what other things his or her proud parents are prepared to pay for, then check out this store. Everything from prams to pushchairs, changing tables to nursery furniture. Also hand-embroidered clothes, as well as the latest from names such as Le Guignol, Sophie Petit, I Pinco Pallino, 1950 and Mariella Ferrari. **Just west of map p. 98, 1A**

**Prenatal** Corso Vercelli 51, corner of Via Cimarosa. Another of the many stores in this popular chain that carries just about everything for young children, babies and mums-to-be. Also Corso Vittorio Emanuele II 13, Corso XXII Marzo 4, Corso Buenos Aires 26, Via Dante 7 and elsewhere. **Just west of map p. 98, 1A**

Shop!

### Futurism

In the early 20th C, bustling, industrial Milan greeted the new world of mechanical force with Futurism, Italy's greatest contribution to modern art. 'A roaring motorcar, its hood adorned with pipes like serpents with explosive breath...is more beautiful than the Winged Victory of Samothrace', declared Futurist theorist Filippo Tommaso Marinetti. He and the other early members of the movement—painters like Umberto Boccioni, Carlo Carrà, Luigi Russolo, Giacomo Balla and Gino Severini—aspired to bring force and movement into art.

The Futurist doctrine of simultaneity, showing successive moments of form in motion, is demonstrated in Boccioni's *Lancers*, below, where the rush of movement is intrinsic to the emotional and compositional heart of the painting. Umberto Boccioni was converted to Futurism in 1908, after he met Carlo Carrà and Emilio Marinetti. Together with Carrà, Russolo, Balla and Severini, he signed the *Technical Manifesto of Futurist Painters* in 1910.

**Umberto Boccioni** *The Charge of the Lancers* (1915)

# PINACOTECA
# AMBROSIANA

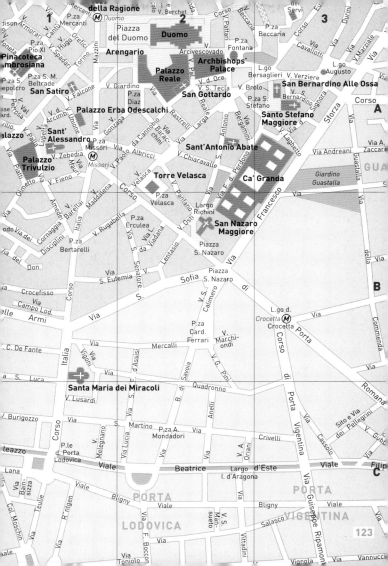

South of the Duomo the monumental aplomb of central Milan ends abruptly around the Pinacoteca Ambrosiana, a superb small art museum. Beyond the museum, the streets grow progressively scruffier as you approach the Navigli, Milan's newest 'bohemian' district. In this formerly neglected part of the city, many of the characteristic houses and courtyards have recently been restored, and now you'll find numerous architects' and designers' studios as well as a selection of fine restaurants. The neighbourhood is particularly lively at night and there is a festival here in June when restaurants are opened on boats.

# Pinacoteca Ambrosiana

| | |
|---|---|
| **OPEN** | The gallery is open 10 am–5.30 pm, Tue–Sun. |
| **CLOSED** | Mon, 1/1, Easter Sunday, 1/5, 25/12 |
| **CHARGES** | Regular admission €7.50; under 18 and over 65 €4.50 |
| **GUIDED VISITS** | Call 02 806 921 |
| **DISABLED ACCESS** | Yes (ask at bookshop) |
| **TELEPHONE** | 02 806 291 |
| **WEB** | www.ambrosiana.it |
| **MAIN ENTRANCE** | Piazza Pio XI 2 |
| **GETTING THERE** | M1 to Duomo/Cordusio or M3 to Duomo |

## HIGHLIGHTS
**Sandro Botticelli's** *Madonna and Child*
**Bergognone's** *Enthroned Madonna*

Bambaia's sculptural fragments from the tomb of Gaston de Foix
Bernardo Luini's *Holy Family with St Anne and the Young St John*
Leonardo da Vinci's *Portrait of a Musician*
Ambrogio de Predis's *Profile of a Young Lady* (Beatrice d'Este)
Jacopo Bassano's *Rest on the Flight into Egypt*
Titian's *Adoration of the Magi*
Caravaggio's *Basket of Fruit*
Raphael's cartoon for the *School of Athens*

The Pinacoteca Ambrosiana first came into being in 1618, created—in accordance with the intentions of its founder, Cardinal Federico Borromeo—as an art academy to promote the aesthetic doctrines of the Council of Trent. The academy itself was founded in 1621, and its first chairman was the painter Giovanni Battista Crespi, known as Il Cerano. The new institution flourished at first, attracting illustrious artists, but later faltered, finally closing in 1776.

What did remain, however, and continued to develop, was the Pinacoteca (or Quadreria), which already included works by Raphael, Leonardo, Luini, Titian, Caravaggio, and Brueghel—the core of the present collection.

The Pinacoteca is arranged in 24 rooms on two floors. The collection is displayed chronologically, though an effort has been made to distinguish Federico Borromeo's original collection.

## BORROMEO COLLECTION I *ROOM 1*

Up the stairs from the entrance to the Pinacoteca one immediately comes to the heart of Federico Borromeo's collection: **Bernardino Luini**'s *Holy Family with St Anne and the Young St John*, from a cartoon by Leonardo, and **Titian**'s *Adoration of the Magi* (painted, with assistants, for Henri II and Diane de Poitiers in 1560, and still in its original frame). There is also a portrait by Titian of an old man in armour, thought to be the artist's father (Gregorio Vecellio, captain of the Centuria di Pieve). The subject of *Profile of a Young Lady* by **Giovanni Ambrogio de Predis**, long believed to be a work of

# PINACOTECA AMBROSIANA

FIRST FLOOR

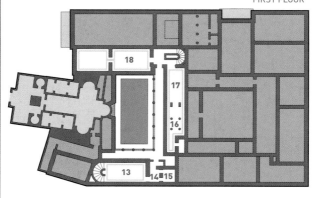

SECOND FLOOR

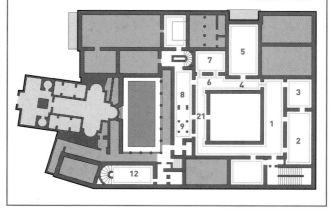

Leonardo, is thought to be Beatrice d'Este, a notable princess of the Este line and wife of Ludovico Sforza, Duke of Milan.

## 15TH–16TH-C ITALIAN AND LOMBARD PAINTINGS
*ROOMS 2–3*

In these two rooms, which host Italian Renaissance paintings that are not part of the Borromeo collection, are several outstanding masterpieces. One such is **Leonardo da Vinci**'s *Portrait of a Musician*: the subject is thought to be Franchino Gaffurio, *maestro di cappella* of Milan cathedral, and the portrait is known for its unprecedented psychological insight.

Other fascinating paintings include **Botticelli**'s light-filled tondo of the *Madonna and Child*, two beautifully painted *Saints* by **Bernardo Zenale**, and **Bergognone**'s great *Sacra Conversazione* (representative of Lombard Quattrocento painting). Among the Leonardo-like paintings are three intriguing works by **Bramantino**: the symbol-laden *Adoration of the Child*, the fresco for the church of San Sepolcro showing *Cristo in Pietà* (witnessed by an extraordinarily expressive St John), and the disquieting altarpiece with the *Madonna Enthroned Between Saints Michael and Ambrose*, with the bodies of a heretic and a toad, symbols of the devil, at their feet.

## BORROMEO COLLECTION II AND III *ROOMS 4–7*

A darkened chamber provides a fit setting for **Raphael**'s cartoon for the *School of Athens*, the only remaining cartoon of the fresco cycle in the Vatican and the largest known Renaissance drawing (285 x 804 cm). The figure of Heraclitus is missing from the cartoon: the Greek philosopher was added by Raphael in the final fresco (he's wearing Michelangelo's face). The other large cartoons in this room were made by **Pellegrino Tibaldi** for the stained glass windows of the Duomo and by **Giulio Romano** for the fresco of the *Battle of Constantine* (also in the Vatican).

Leaving the Raphael room it's easy to miss **Caravaggio**'s *Basket of Fruit* (see picture on p. 128). Cardinal Borromeo was aware of

**Caravaggio** *Basket of Fruit* (1597)

the value of this extraordinary still life, as is clear from his complaint that there was no painting worthy to be placed beside it. Caravaggio was a native of Lombardy and trained there before going off to Rome, where he achieved recognition (but was often in trouble with the authorities because of his violent temper; he fled Rome after killing a man in a fight over a wager on tennis).

Only two of the four allegories of the elements painted by **Jan Brueghel** for the Cardinal and removed by Napoleon in 1796 remain st the Ambrosiana. These are *Water* and the enigmatic *Fire*, a rather fiendish forge full of tiny pieces of goldsmith's work. Brueghel also painted the life-sized vase of flowers with jewels, coins and shells, a superb example of this kind of still life, and the little painting on copper of a mouse with roses.

The other Flemish painter whose work Cardinal Borromeo supported is **Paul Brill**, here represented by a number of meticulously detailed religious landscapes. The German printmaker **Luca di Leida** made the grisly monochrome painting on glass of the *Triumph of David*, with Goliath's colossal head carried on his sword.

## PAINTINGS AND OBJETS D'ART OF THE 14TH–16TH CENTURIES *ROOMS 8–9*

The *Sala della Medusa* and *Sala delle Colonne* hold an important collection of objets d'art, including Milanese daggers, small objects made from ivory, metal and crystal and a curious profane reliquary with a lock of Lucrezia Borgia's hair.

## 16TH-C ITALIAN PAINTINGS *ROOM 12*

The Venetian, Northern Italian and Tuscan painters represented in these rooms include **Jacopo Bassano**, whose *Rest on the Flight into Egypt* hangs here.

In the *Sala dell'Esedra*, decorated in 1930 with a mosaic reproducing the miniature made by by Simone Martini for Petrarch's personal copy of Virgil (preserved in the library), are works by painters from Bergamo and Brescia. **Moretto**'s dramatic *Martyrdom of St Peter of Verona*, in which the martyr writes on the ground, in his own blood, *credo* ('I believe'), and **Giovanni Battista Moroni**'s remarkable full-length *Portrait of Michel de l'Hopital*, French ambassador to the Coucil of Trent, are perhaps the most striking.

## 16TH- AND 17TH-C ITALIAN AND FLEMISH PAINTINGS *ROOM 13*

On the first floor in the *Sala Nicolò da Bologna* and in the next room are Italian and Flemish works, including **Guido Reni**'s *Penitent Magdalene*, represented kneeling holding a skull; one of **Evaristo Baschenis**' celebrated still lifes of musical instruments; and **Giuseppe Vermiglio**'s beautiful *Judith with the Head of Holofernes*.

## 17TH- AND 18TH-C LOMBARD AND ITALIAN PAINTINGS, THE DE PECIS COLLECTION *ROOM 14–18*

Among the paintings that mark the passage from the 17th to the 18th centuries are *Portrait of a Young Man* (the subject seemingly caught by surprise) by **Fra Galgario** and the stiff official *Portrait of Leopold II of Habsburg Lorraine* by **Anton Raphael Mengs**.

A recently opened room holds a selection of works from the De Pecis collection, given to the Ambrosiana in 1827. The collection includes several 19th-C miniatures on ivory by **Giambattista Gigola** and the beautiful portrait of the French dancer Carolina Pitrot Angiolini painted by **Andrea Appiani**.

## 15TH- AND 16TH-C FLEMISH AND GERMAN PAINTINGS, SCULPTURE AND FRESCOES *ROOM 21*

The last two rooms on the first floor, overlooking the great reading room of the library, hold an important group of 16th-C Flemish and German paintings and sculpture (partly from the De Pecis collection). The works range from Roman and Lombard fragments to reliefs by sculptor **Bambaia** for the unfinished tomb of Gaston de Foix (1515-22; other pieces of the tomb are in the Museo d'Arte Antica, Castello Sforzesco, see p. 63).

## THE LIBRARY

The famous library, founded by Cardinal Borromeo (who is a major character in *I Promessi Sposi*), contains about 750,000 volumes, including 3,000 incunabula and 35,000 manuscripts. Among the more precious works are Arabic and Syriac manuscripts; a *Divine Comedy* (1353); Petrarch's own copy of Virgil, illuminated by Simone Martini; the *Codice Atlantico*, a collection of Leonardo's drawings on scientific and artistic subjects; a printed Virgil (Venice, 1470); and a Boccaccio (1471).

# San Lorenzo, Sant'Eustorgio and the Museo Diocesano

| | |
|---|---|
| **OPEN** | The churches are open 8 am–12 pm and 2.30 pm–6 pm. The Museo Diocesano is open 10 am–6 pm, Tues-Sun, and 10 am–8 pm on Thur. |
| **CLOSED** | *Museo Diocesano* Mon and all of Aug |
| **CHARGES** | Regular admission to the Museo Diocesano €8.50; under 18 and over 60 €6. Cumulative ticket with Pinacoteca Ambrosiana and Museo del Duomo €12. Cumulative ticket to the Museo Diocesano, Basilica di Sant'Eustorgio and Cappella Portinari, Basilica di San Lorenzo and Cappella di Sant'Aquilino €12; under 18 and over 60 €7.50. |
| **GUIDED VISITS** | Museo Diocesano Audio guides; English-language guide available on request at 02 8942 0019, 02 659 8885. Dopocena al museo, third Thur of every month: concert, tea and cakes, guided visits with the Museum Director. |
| **DISABLED ACCESS** | Yes |
| **SERVICES** | Bookshop, café |
| **TELEPHONE** | *Museo Diocesano* 02 8940 4714 |
| **WEB** | www.museodiocesano.it |
| **MAIN ENTRANCE** | *Museo Diocesano* Corso di Porta Ticinese 95 |
| **GETTING THERE** | M2 to Sant'Ambrogio/Sant'Agostino |

## HIGHLIGHTS

**Roman colonnade**      San Lorenzo Maggiore
**Roman architecture and antiquities**
**Roman palaeo-Christian Chapel of Sant'Aquilino**

**12th–13th C architecture**      Sant'Eustorgio
**Renaissance Cappella Portinari**
**High altar with jewel-encrusted 9th-C gold and silver casing**

| | |
|---|---|
| Vincenzo Foppa's frescoes of the *Life of St Peter Martyr* | Sant'Eustorgio |
| Bergognone's *St Catherine of Alexandria* | Museo Diocesano |
| Gold-ground paintings | |
| Gaetano Previati's frescoes of the Stations of the Cross | |

# SAN LORENZO MAGGIORE

Sixteen Corinthian columns, the remains of a Roman portico erected in the 4th C, are an imposing reminder of just how old Milan really is. Behind this striking colonnade rises one of the favourite churches of the Milanese, the basilica of San Lorenzo Maggiore. Founded in the 4th C, it was rebuilt after the collapse of the vault in 1103 and again in 1574–88, but preserves the original octagonal form and much of the original masonry. The exterior presents four heavy square towers and a façade added on in 1894.

## INTERIOR

The spacious domed interior, built of grey stone, is surrounded by an ambulatory beneath a gallery. The Chapel of Sant'Aquilino was built in the 4th C, probably as an imperial mausoleum. In the vestibule (there is a light on the right) are fragments of 5th-C mosaics and early-14th-C frescoes. The doorjambs (1st–3rd C AD) were brought from a Roman building. The octagonal hall, a remarkable Roman room, contains an early Christian sarcophagus and two lunettes with 5th-C mosaics. Beyond is a 17th C silver urn with the relics of the 7th-C Milanese martyr St Aquilinus, set beneath a little frescoed vault. Steps behind it lead down to an undercroft with Roman masonry of the imperial period, probably once part of an amphitheatre.

Corso di Porta Ticinese continues south from San Lorenzo, passing through the arches of the medieval Porta Ticinese (c. 1330) at Via Mulino delle Armi. To the east is the quiet, green

Parco delle Basiliche, which links San Lorenzo with the area's other great medieval church, Sant'Eustorgio, and provides an alternative route between the two monuments.

## SANT'EUSTORGIO

Sant'Eustorgio is also of ancient foundation, an 11th-C church mostly rebuilt in the 12th–13th C and with a façade reconstructed in 1863–65. The three 15th-C chapels on the south side, the apse, the slender campanile (1297–1309), and the graceful Portinari chapel, are easy to see from the outside. To the left of the façade is a 16th-C open-air pulpit.

## INTERIOR

The long, low interior, with aisles and apse, is typical of the Lombard basilica, but an important series of chapels was added on the south side from the 13th to the 16th centuries. The first

Sant'Eustorgio

chapel dates from 1484, and has good sculptural detail and an altarpiece by **Bergognone**. There are tombs of the Viscontis in the second, fourth and sixth chapels, and in the south transept is the chapel of the Magi, where the relics of the Magi were preserved until their transfer to Cologne in 1164 (some were returned to Milan in 1903). It contains the huge Roman sarcophagus that held the relics, and on the high altar is a finely carved 14th-C stone dossal.

Across the confessio, with nine slender monolithic columns (above early Christian foundations), and beneath the raised apse, is the Cappella Portinari (1462–68), a beautiful Renaissance chapel built for Pigello Portinari and dedicated to St Peter Martyr (a Veronese inquisitor murdered in 1252 by supporters of the Manichaean heresy). A graceful choir of angels with festoons in coloured stucco plays over the drum of the dome. The frescoed scenes of the *Life of St Peter Martyr*, by **Vincenzo Foppa** (1466–68), comprise the most important Renaissance fresco cycle in the city (unfortunately, they are in very poor condition). In the centre is the tomb, borne by eight Virtues, of St Peter Martyr himself, sculpted in 1339.

The sacristy shows the early Christian cemetery beneath the nave, with tombs dating from the 1st–4th centuries AD.

## MUSEO DIOCESANO

The Museum of the Diocese of Milan opened in 2001 in the second cloister of the basilica of Sant'Eustorgio. It documents the importance of local Christianity, from the time of St Ambrose (334-397) to the present. The plan for the renovation of the monastery was created in 1987 by the architectural firm Studio Belgiojoso; the installation was designed in 1996 by architects Antonio and Michele Piva.

The visit begins with **WORKS FROM THE MUSEUM OF THE BASILICA DI SANT'AMBROGIO**. Most interesting, for historical as well as aesthetic reasons, are the large 10th-C stucco tondo with

**Bergognone** *Santa Caterina d'Alessandria*

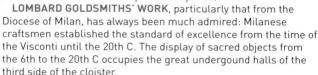

the *Bust of St Ambrose* and the fragments from the wooden main door of the Basilica of Sant'Ambrogio (see p. 100), which date from the 4th or 5th C. Of the paintings from the various parishes of the Diocese of Milan, the best are Anovelo da Imbonate's *Crucifixion*, Alessandro Magnasco's *Il furto sacrilego*, and **Bergognone**'s *St Catherine of Alexandria* (see picture on p. 135).

**LOMBARD GOLDSMITHS' WORK**, particularly that from the Diocese of Milan, has always been much admired: Milanese craftsmen established the standard of excellence from the time of the Visconti until the 20th C. The display of sacred objects from the 6th to the 20th C occupies the great undergound halls of the third side of the cloister.

The large **SALONE DELL'ARCICONFRATERNITA DEL SANTISSIMO SACRAMENTO** hosts a cycle of paintings commissioned by the Arciconfraternita, dedicated to miracles of the Eucharist and to their patron saint, St Catherine. The large canvases were commissioned in the late 17th C from the most important painters in Milan. The recovery of these valuable works, finally restored and made visible after decades of neglect, introduces the visitor to the confraternities—which played an important religious and social role in the Milanese diocese.

**GOLD-GROUND PAINTING** is one of the fundamental categories of mediaeval Italian religious art. The 41 panels in this gathering were executed in the 14th and 15th centuries, mainly in Tuscany and Umbria. Among the principal artists represented are Gerardo di Jacopo and the Florentine Bernardo Daddi.

The 172 paintings and drawings that made up the private **COLLECTION OF CARDINAL GESARE MONTI** (1593-1650) constitute the first core of the Milanese archbishops' collections. The cardinal's tastes, perfectly aligned with the spirit of the Counter Reformation, are oriented toward the 16th-C Venetian school, the early 17th-C Lombard painters and the Emilian school. Among the more remarkable works that Monti left to the diocese are Bernardino Lanino's *Salvator Mundi*; Cerano's *Fall of St Paul*; **Tintoretto**'s *Christ and the Adulteress* and Simone Peterzano's *Christ in the Garden*.

The paintings in the **POZZOBONELLI COLLECTION,** left to the diocese by Cardinal Giuseppe Pozzobonelli (1696-1783), point to the artistic cult of Arcadia—the representation of idealized landscapes, with and without figures, that spread through Milan in the 18th C. Among the most interesting works on display are those by Giovanni Paolo Panini, Francesco Zuccarelli and Pieter Mulier. The Visconti collection, in contrast, is a complex collection, put together at different times; it shows the increasing interest in 17th-C Lombard art that Cardinal Federico Visconti developed. Although it contains roughly 40 paintings and drawings, only three works are hung, including **Cerano**'s little panel painting of *St Charles in Glory.* The collection of Benedetto Erba Odescalchi (1679-1740), who was appointed Archbishop of Milan in 1712, is a series of 41 portraits of Milanese bishop saints. *St Barnabas* and *St Castriziano* (both by anonymous 18th-C Lombard painters) are particularly good.

**GAETANO PREVIATI'S STATIONS OF THE CROSS** (1882-1888) from the cemetery of Castano Primo show a firm command of the Symbolist movement that had developed north of the Alps. The third station, where Christ falls for the first time, and the fourth station, where Jesus encounters his mother, are particularly moving. Previati is best known for his paintings of the rural working class.

# in the area

**San Satiro** Via Spadari leads from the Pinocoteca Ambrosiana to the busy Via Torino, across which is the beautiful church of San Satiro. You can see the exterior, with a campanile of the mid-11th C, from Via Falcone. The church was rebuilt by in 1478 b y Bramante. The T-shaped interior, by a clever perspective device and the skilful use of stucco, has the appearance of a Greek cross, although the rear wall is actually almost flat. The eight-sided baptistery is a beautiful Renaissance work, with terracottas by Fondutis on a design by Bramante. **Map p. 123, 1A**

**Palazzo Erba Odescalchi** This fine 16th-C palace, off Via Torino, at Via Unione 5, is now a police station. It has a remarkable elliptical spiral staircase that is attributed by some scholars to Bramante. **Map p. 123, 2A**

**Santo Stefano Maggiore** and **San Bernardino alle Osse** Just a couple of blocks southeast of Piazza del Duomo, beyond Via Larga, is the deconsecrated church of Santo Stefano Maggiore, a Baroque building (1584–95) with a later campanile. Galeazzo Maria Sforza was murdered in 1476 outside the building that stood on this spot. In the same piazza is the church of San Bernardino alle Osse, with an ossuary chapel frescoed by Sebastiano Ricci. **Map p. 123, 3A**

**Sant'Antonio Abate** Near Ca' Granda on Via Sant'Antonio you can see the 12th-C campanile of Sant'Antonio Abate, a church of 1582 with a 12th-C campanile and 17th-C choir stalls. Adjoining it (Via Sant'Antonio 5) is a charming cloister of the early 16th C. **Map p. 123, 2A**

**Ca' Granda** Fronting Via Festa del Perdono is the huge building of the former Ospedale Maggiore, or Ca' Granda, which has been the headquarters of the University of Milan since 1958. The hospital was founded by Francesco Sforza in 1456. The building was designed by Filarete with two matching wings, one for men and one for women. The long façade on Via Festa del Perdono preserves the 15th-C wing at the right-hand end, with terracotta decorations; the left-hand end, in Neoclassical style, dates from 1797–1804. The huge collection of paintings that belonged to the hospital includes portraits of benefactors from 1602 onwards, by the best-known artists of the day. **Map p. 123, 3A**

**San Nazaro Maggiore** The basilica of San Nazaro Maggiore, the easternmost of the four churches founded by St Ambrose outside the walls, was consecrated in 386. It was reconstructed after a fire of 1075, altered in the late 16th C and restored in the 20th C after war damage. The entrance on Corso di Porta Romana is preceded by the hexagonal Trivulzio Chapel, with an elegant plain interior and uniform family tombs in niches high up on the walls.

The interior of the church preserves, in part, the plan of the early Christian basilica—and some of its masonry. In the nave are paintings by Camillo Procaccini and Daniele Crespi and the architecture of the crossing is particularly fine. In the south transept is a *Last Supper* by Bernardino Lanino. The sanctuary preserves the reconstructed dedication stone (with two original fragments), and off the south side, the

**Torre Velasca**

little 10th-C Chapel of St Lino (restored in 1948). In the north transept you can see a 16th-C carved-wood Gothic tabernacle with the *Nativity*, very well preserved; a reconstructed funerary epitaph (435); and a painting by Bernardino Luini. The Chapel of St Catherine also has frescoes by Luini. **Map p. 123, 2B**

**Torre Velasca** Off the busy Corso di Porta Romana rises this curiously medieval-looking skyscraper, built in 1956–58. Designed by Studio BBPR (Banfi, Belgiojoso, Peressuti and Rogers), it is one of the most important Modern buildings in the city. **Map p. 123, 2A**

**Museo Francesco Messina** In the ex-church of San Sisto (Via San Sisto 4) is a museum of the works of 20th-C realist sculptor Francesco Messina (open 9.30 am–1 pm, Tues–Sun; 02 8645 3005). **Map p. 122, 3A**

**Santa Maria dei Miracoli** The church, also known as Santa Maria presso San Celso, stands next to a pretty little garden in front of San Celso. In the dark interior is a *Holy Family* by Paris Bordone; statues by Annibale Fontana and Stoldo Lorenzi adorn the dome piers. The inlaid choir stalls are by Galeazzo Alessi, and the ambulatory has altarpieces by Gaudenzio

**Antiques for sale on the Navigli**

Ferrari and Moretto. In the north aisle is an altarpiece by Bergognone.
**Map p. 122, 1B**

**Porta Ticinese** Just south of Sant'Eustorgio is the huge Piazza XXIV
Maggio, with the handsome Neoclassical Porta Ticinese, an Ionic
gateway by Luigi Cagnola (1801–14), in the centre. To the west is the
Darsena, once the port of Milan, which was connected to an extensive
system of rivers and canals. **Map p. 122, 3C**

**Navigli** A working-class neighbourhood for eight hundred years, the
Navigli quarter developed around two medieval canals. The Naviglio
Grande, which linked the port of Milan to the River Ticino, 50 km away,
was begun in the 12th C and was navigable as far as Milan by the 13th C.
It carried commodities to and from the city, and there was a regular
passenger service along it from the beginning of the 19th C. The nearby
Naviglio Pavese was built as an irrigation canal from Milan to Pavia by
Gian Galeazzo Visconti in the 14th C. Today this is a vibrant
neighbourhood, home to a number of artists' studios and plenty of
restaurants, bars and cafés. **Map p. 122, 1–2C**

# commercial galleries

**Arte 92** Via Moneta 1a, 02 805 2347, fax 02 805 3110, www.arte92.it. Rafael Canogar, Lucio Del Pezzo, Hans Hartung, Alberto Magnelli, André Masson, Georges Mathieu, Vittorio Mattino, Mimmo Paladino, Arnulf Rainer, Mimmo Rotella and Emilio Scanavino. **Map 123, 1A**

**Massimo Carasi** Via Vaina 2, 02 5831 3809, fax 02 58313809, www.carasi.it. Luca Francesconi, Gretta Frau, Leonardo Greco, Andrea Mastrovito, Kristofer Paetau, Mario Rizzi, Kirstine Roepstorff. **Map p. 123, 3C**

**Maria Cilena** Via Ariberto 17, 02 8323521. International contemporary art, especially by younger artists. **Map p. 122, 2B**

**Emi Fontana** Viale Bligny 42, 02 5832 2237, fax 02 5832 2237. Fresh contemporary art. **Map p. 123, 2C**

**Pasquale Leccese** Via Circo 1, 02 7201 6262. International contemporary art, especially by younger artists. **Map p. 122, 3A**

**Laura Pecci** Via Bocconi 9, 02 5843 0047, fax 02 5843 4287, www.gallerialaurapecci.com. International contemporary art, especially by younger artists. **Map p. 123, 2C**

# eat

**€€ Alla Collina Pistoiese** Via Amedei 1, near Piazza Missori, 02 877248. Not to be confused with Colline Senesi, which is in another part of town entirely. This traditional-style Tuscan restaurant has been here since 1938. Despite the name, you can get risotto and *cotoletta alla milanese*, and although this place is closed all day Fri and Sat lunch, it is open on Sundays—unlike most restaurants in Milan. Also closed Dec 25–Jan 6, Easter and all of Aug. **Map p. 123, 1A**

**Hostaria Borromei** Via Borromei 4, 02 8645 3760. This restaurant offers you a chance to sample the cuisine of the Mantua area. Given its proximity to the exchange, the restaurant caters to a lot of business people at lunch. In the summer months (except Aug 8–13, when the restaurant is closed) the pretty courtyard becomes the dining area. Closed Sat lunchtime and all day Sun, as well as between Christmas and Jan 6. **Map p. 122, 3A**

**Trattoria Milanese** Via Santa Marta 11, 02 8645 1991. While the city has seen many changes, this area still has an old-time feel, and indeed the Trattoria Milanese has run by the same family since 1913. The menu has not changed in 50 years, they say, so this is the place to try the old-fashioned *risotto giallo* (with saffron), *mondeghili alla verza*, *nervetti* and *cotoletta milanese*. Closed Tue, and from mid-July to the end of Aug. **Map p. 122, 3A**

€€€**Cracco-Peck** Via Victor Hugo 4, 02 876774. Located in the food lover's haven that lies between the Duomo and the Ambrosiana (see store listing on p. 145), Peck has long been one of Milan's legendary gourmet restaurants. When Carlo Cracco joined as the new chef in January 2001, his name was added to the marquee. It did not take long for him to make his mark: Cracco-Peck made the two-star Michelin grade for 2004. The setting is sophisticated, crafted from wood and marble, leather chairs and silver trays, and the menu consists of creative interpretations of traditional dishes. These include risotto with anchovy-flavoured oil, lemon and a dash of cocoa; ravioli stuffed with goat's milk and spugnole mushrooms; and lobster in a casserole with broccoli, tiny corn-on-the-cob and pecorino. Closed Sat lunchtimes,

Sun, Dec 22–Jan 10 and Aug 10–31. Reservations essential. **Map p. 122, 3A**

## CAFÉS

€ **Gelateria Ecologica Artigiana** Corso Porta Ticinese 40, close to the corner with Via de Amicis. Be prepared to queue, and don't bother looking for vanilla—they won't have it. Instead try some of the unusual flavours, such as sesame-honey or date. Closed Wed. **Map p. 122, 3B**

**Caffe Vergnano** Via Speronari 3, 02 86996858. This café and gelateria has a pretty little courtyard that backs onto the walls of the church of San Satiro (see p. 137). Just five tables. **Map p. 123, 2B**

€€ **Spadari** Via Spadari, on the corner of Via Cantù. This and Café Victor Hugo, across the street, are two of the better places in the city for a quick lunch; Spadari has a wider selection of sandwiches, while Victor Hugo has more hot dishes. **Map p. 123, 1A**

**Victor Hugo** Via Spadari, on the corner of Via Cantù. Though a bit pricey, the light lunches are good and the ambience, elegant yet comfortable. **Map p. 123, 1A**

# shop

**The two main shopping streets in this area are actually two parts of one main way. Via Torino runs from the Duomo, then at Carrobbio it becomes Corso di Porta Ticinese, which extends all the way into Piazza XXIV Maggio. (Where the actual Porta Ticinese stands—see p. 140.) The mood of these streets is young, if not inexpensive.**

## CLOTHING

**B-Fly** Corso di Porta Ticinese 46. This Levi's cult store is more like a museum than a clothing shop. Includes the Levi's Vintage and Red Line collections. **Map p. 122, 3B**

**Biffi** Corso Genova 6. Mrs Biffi has been sourcing cutting-edge designs for the last twenty years. The current selection for women includes Yohji Yamamoto, Gucci, Jean Paul Gaultier, Donna Karan, Helmut Lang, Marni, Martin Margiela and Bottega Veneta. Menwswear options include Yohji Yamamoto, Gucci, Donna Karan and Paul Smith. **Map p. 122, 2B**

**Diesel** Corso di Porta Ticinese 44 89420916. At this concept store, check out the prototype versions of Diesel jeans, or pick your favourite styles and have them custom-made. Just down the street at Porta Ticinese 75, see the 55DSL line. Then check what's featured on the 'Diesel wall' to the right of the church of San Lorenzo. If you're interested, look at www.diesel.com to find out how to get your own message up there. **Map p. 122, 3B**

**Energie** Via Torino 19. If you're feeling energetic, sample all five floors of this young, trendy streetwear shop. As well as Energie, there's also Killah Babe and Miss Sixty. **Map p. 123, 1A**

**Fatto a Mano** Corso di Porta Ticinese 76. Silk, taffeta, and shantung for shirts, trousers, dresses and beaded purses and belts, inspired by the Far East. Also at Via Ponte Vetero 19. **Map p. 122, 3B**

**Fornarina** Corso di Porta Ticinese 78. Hot stuff for the younger crowd. **Map p. 122, 3B**

**Martino Midali** Corso di Porta Ticinese 60. Knitwear for all seasons, as well as tailored and more casual clothing, including some roomier styles under the Midali Toujours label. Also at Via Ponte Vetero 9. **Map p. 122, 3B**

**No Season** Corso di Porta Ticinese 77. This lifestyle emporium for modern urbanites has clothing, shoes, books, music, perfume and housewares. As well as Antonio Berardi, Helmut Lang, Jean Paul Gaultier and Vivienne Westwood, there are plenty of sporty brands, including Adidas, Nike and Puma. **Map p. 122, 3B**

**Plus** Piazza Missori 2. Top-name designer labels including Philosophy by Alberta Ferretti, Marithé & François Girbaud, and Jean Paul Gaultier, as well as knitwear by Gentry Portofino, Fuzzi and Liviana Conti. **Map p. 123, 1A**

**ProMod** Via Mazzini 2. If you are comfortable with the help-yourself Etam and Topshop type of store, then this French women's ready-to-wear and accessories chain with its affordable prices is for you. Also in Corso Buenos Aires, corner of Via Vitruvio. **Map p. 123, 1A**

**Taboo** Piazza Generale Cantore 3. Located at the Navigli end of Corso Genova, this fun fashion store offers quirky collections from Daniele Bizzi and Kristina Ti, along with raku ceramics, candles and a selection of jewellery. **Map p. 122, 2B**

**Zeus** Corso Genova 24. Another trendy boutique for romantic, feminine ready-to-wear, lingerie and swimwear: Blugirl, Blumarine, Just Cavalli, Paola Frani and Plein Sud. **Map p. 122, 2B**

## MARKET INTELLIGENCE

Complementing the shopping streets are two markets, both held on Saturday.

**Viale Papiniano**, or at least the piece that runs from Piazzale Cantore—where Corso Genova meets the Darsena (**Map p. 122, 2B**)—to Piazza Sant'Agostino, becomes a huge street market on Sat: a crowded favourite of locals and visitors alike. It starts about 8.30 am and goes on until about 5 pm, with great bargains to be had on designer wear. Watch out for pickpockets. There is a smaller version on Tue through to about 2 pm.

The second market is the **Fiera di Sinigallia**. Located on the Viale Gabriele d'Annunzio side of the Darsena, this is more of a flea-market and ethnic knick-knack market.

## THE HOME

**MDF** Via della Chiusa, corner of Via Crocefisso. Contemporary designer furniture. There are several other furniture stores in the area between San Lorenzo and Via Torino. Take a stroll! **Map p. 123, 1B**

**Frette** Via Torino 42. Top-of-the-line household linens. Also at Corso Buenos Aires, corner of Via Pecchio, Corso Vercelli 23-25, Via Manzoni 11. **Map p. 123, 1A**

## FOOD

**Peck** Via Spadari 9. Peck is, quite simply, three levels' worth of the best that Italy can offer in terms of food and wine. Upstairs is a café and gift store where you can find something for that foodie in your life (try the chocolate and pistachio spread); on the ground floor is the main shop, with beautiful cuts of meat, cheeses, pasta and more; below is a wine cellar. **Map p. 123, 1A**

Although Peck is the best, Via Victor Hugo and Via Spadari, with Via Speronari, its continuation on the other side of Via Torino, have a wide array of food shops. The **Casa del Formaggio**, at Via Speronari 3, features cheeses from all parts of Italy. **Princi**, at Via Speronari 6, is a bakery and café. Almost next door is the **Enoteca Vino Vino** at No. 4, which carries over 1,000 red and white wines as well as sparkling wines, grappa and distilled liqueurs—and 23 types of honey. **Giovanni Galli Marroni e Canditi**, at Via Victor Hugo 2, makes delicious and beautiful candies and sweets.

**Funghi for sale at Peck**

# entertainment

**INFORMATION
TICKETS
VENUES
NIGHTLIFE
TOURS
FESTIVALS
THEATRES**

In general, Italy is a home-loving nation. Even in Milan, considered the nightlife capital of Italy, people are more likely to spend comfortable evenings in with their friends and family and there's not a bar or club scene like in London or New York. Those who do go out tend to be quite young, but are not heavy drinkers.

## WHERE TO GET INFORMATION

For information on concerts, theatre and live music consult *HelloMilano*, a free magazine available in hotels and at the APT information office (**Map p. 8, 3C**) in Piazza del Duomo. www.hellomilano.it

*Milano Mese* is a monthly magazine available free of charge at APT offices or online at www.milanoinfotourist.com.

Milan's citizens read about events in *ViviMIlano,* which is given away with the Wednesday edition of the national daily *Corriere della Sera*, or in *TutttoMilano*, which is available with the Thursday edition of daily paper *La Repubblica*.

## TICKETS

**Biglietteria** Corso Garibaldi 81, 02 659 0188 **Map p. 52, 3A**

**Box Office** (www.boxoffice.it) provides advance booking and ticket sales for many events. Downstairs at the Ricordi Media Store, Galleria V. Emanuele, 02 869 0683, **Map p. 8, 2B**

The **tourist office** (APT) at Piazza del Duomo (**Map p. 8, 3C**) sells a few tickets for some of the more popular classical music associations.

## VENUES
## BALLET AND OPERA

**Teatro alla Scala** Piazza della Scala, 02 7200 3744. La Scala, possibly the most famous opera house in the world, was closed for renovation at the time of writing, and the theatre's ballet and opera programmes were being staged at the Teatro degli Arcimboldi Viale dell'Innovazione, 02 7200 3744. **Map p. 8, 2B**

## CLASSICAL

**Auditorium di Milano** Largo Gustav Mahler, 02 8338 9201/03. Off the map. Home to Milan's symphony orchestra and the Stagione Sinfonica concert series.

**Conservatorio di Musica Giuseppe Verdi** Via Conservatorio 12, 02 762 1101. Home to the Orchestra da Camera della Lombardia; Serate Musicali, Società dei Concerti, Società del Quartetto concert series. **Map p. 9, 2C**

**Musica e Poesia a San Maurizio** Classical music concerts in Milanese churches throughout the year; 02 7600 5500. One of their series is an excellent early music program with internationally renowned artists. The frescoed chapel at San Maurizio itself is superb. **Map p. 98, 3B**

## JAZZ

**Blue Note** Via Borsieri 37, 02 6085 6199. Off the map. This jazz club is Milan's top place and pretty much the only one worth visiting. It offers two sets of great live music every evening, simple but refined food and a Sun brunch with music. It's actually an expansion—the first European one—of the famous NYC Blue Note. To see Italian artists, make sure to come on a Mon.

**Osteria del Jazz** Via F. Carcano 8, 02 469 4861. Off the map. Live jazz, plus a vast assortment of wines and simple food.

**Scimmie** Via Ascanio Sforza 49, 02 8940 2874. Off the map. Live jazz and blues every night; good Italian and French food. It also hosts an English-language stand-up comedy night with local and visiting comedians on Wed and Thur.

## LATE NIGHT

**ATM** Bastioni di Porta Volta 15, 02 655 2365. Off the map. Formerly a bus station, now a popular bar. Closed Sun.

**Birrificio di Lambrate** Via Adelchi 5, 02 7063 8678. Off the map. The first in Milan to produce its own (excellent) beers.

**Bodeguita del Medio** Viale Col di Lana 3, 02 8940 0560. Off the map. A taste of Cuba: Cuban dishes, good selection of rums, live music. Closed Sun.

**Camparino Bar Zucca** Piazza del Duomo 21, 02 8646 4435. A Milanese institution, open late and tranquil: antique furnishings, tables in the Vittorio Emanuele Arcade and a tea room. **Map p. 8, 3C**

**Cuore** Via G. G. Mora 3, 02 5810 5126. Avant-garde design, lots of levels, lots of disco. **Map 122, 3B**

**Gattopardo Café** Via Piero della Francesca 47, 02 3453 7699. Off the map. Disco in a former church; sometimes hard to get in. It's got a beautiful chandelier in the middle and informal happy hour that extends (happily) into the wee hours.

**Julien Café** Via C. M. Maggi 6, 02 349 0459. Popular café with copper walls and jazz. Closed Sun. **Map p. 52, 2A**

**L'Atlantique** Viale Umbria 42, 02 5519 3925. Off the map. This hi-tech bar is one of Milan's most known night spots and can be hard to get into.

**Stonehedge** Viale Pasubio 3, 02 655 2846. Off the map. Inevitably, even Milan has a Celtic-esque pub, and it's quite popular.

## GAY- & LESBIAN-FRIENDLY

**After Line Disco Pub** Via Sammartini 25, 02 669 2130. Off the map. Very popular gay disco.

**Birreria Uno Alternativa** Via Borsieri 14, 02 6900 3271. Off the map. Gay and lesbian beer parlour, with an internet station at every table to chat.

**Cicip e Ciciap** Via Gorani 9, 02 877555. Restaurant and club for women only; closed Mon. **Map p. 98, 1B**

**G-Lounge** Via Larga 8, 02 805 3042. Stylish interior design and sophisticated music; one of the trendiest gay bars in town. Open Thur–Sat. **Map p. 8, 3C**

**Recycle** Via Calabria 5, 02 376 1531. Off the map. One of Milan's first lesbian bars. Fri–Sun for women; open to everyone on Wed–Thur.

**Sottomarino Giallo** Via Donatello 2, 339 545 4127. Disco for women only, open to general public on Wed and Fri. **Map p. 84, 3A**

## SPECIAL EVENTS

**January**
*Corteo dei Re Magi* Procession of the Magi from the Duomo to the basílica of Sant'Eustorgio, with elaborate costumes and street music.

**February**
*Carnevale Ambrosiano* Masks and floats throughout the city until the first Saturday of Lent

**March**
*MODIT – Milanovendemoda* Presentation of the autumn-winter fashion collections

*Milano – Sanremo* Bicycle race

**April**
*Fiera dei Fiori* Flower fair on Via Moscova, Whit Monday.

*Bagutta-Pittori* Open air art exhibition on Via Bagutta, third week of the month

**May**
*Cortili Aperti* Courtyards and gardens of historic palaces opened to the public by the Associazione Dimore Storiche Italiane (02 954 7311)

**June**
*Festa del Naviglio* Open market, street theatre and musical events around the Naviglio Grande, first Sun of the month

**July-August**
*Festival Latino Americano* South American music and cuisine at the Forum d'Assago

*Arianteo* Open-air cinema at the Rotonda della Besana

**September**
*Gran Premio di Monza* Formula 1 Grand Prix at the Monza racetrack, near Milan

**October**
*Smau* Computer and multimedia technologies fair

*MODIT - Milanovendemoda* Presentation of spring-summer fashion collections

**November**
*Premio Bagutta* Literary prize ceremony

**December**
*Sant' Ambrogio* Feast day of Milan's patron saint (Dec 7); 'Bej Oh Bej' street fair near Sant'Ambrogio (see p. 117) and opening night at Teatro alla Scala

# planning

**WHEN TO GO**
**HOW TO GET AROUND**
**PRACTICALITIES**
**FOOD AND DRINK**
**PLACES TO STAY**

## WHEN TO GO

The best time to visit Milan is late spring (May–June) or early autumn (September–October). The city is known for later autumn months that are often wet and unexpectedly chilly, with strong northerly winds. The height of the summer is unpleasantly hot, and winter days are sometimes as cold and wet as in Britain.

Milan is a business-oriented city, with a steady stream of important trade fairs on everything from fashion to consumer electronics. The biggest event of all is the furniture fair, which runs in the second week of April each year. Most attendees book accommodation far in advance, so if you're in town while a fair is on you'll find it very difficult to find a hotel room, taxi or table in a restaurant. But don't despair—advance planning is all you need.

Don't forget that Milan, like all working cities in Italy, closes down in August as most residents (including hoteliers and restaurateurs) head for the hills or the shores. A visitor to the city during this season will not only find it unbearably hot and humid, but your first-choice accommodation may not be available. Also, beware of long weekends (*'ponti'*) and the extraordinarily short work week between April 25 (Liberation Day) and May 1 (Labour Day).

## PASSPORTS AND FORMALITIES

Passports or ID cards are necessary for EU travellers entering Italy; North American travellers must carry passports. For visits of up to 90 days no visa is required for EU, US or Canadian citizens holding a valid passport. Citizens of other countries should check current visa requirements with the nearest Italian consulate before departure.

Italian law requires travellers to carry some form of identification at all times. All foreign visitors to Italy must register with the police within three days of arrival. If you are staying at a hotel, this formality is attended to by the management. If staying with friends or in a private home, you must register in person at the nearest police station (*questura*).

# GETTING THERE
## BY AIR

Milan is served by two airports: **Malpensa**, 45 km northwest, for international and domestic flights, and **Linate**, 7 km east, for a few international and domestic flights and the shuttle to Rome. The same firm manages both airports (02 7485 2200, www.sea-aeroportimilano.it).

Bergamo's **Orio al Serio** airport, 45 km east of Milan, also has direct flights to/from domestic and European cities and is a favourite of low-cost airlines (035 326323, www.orioaeroporto.it).

### BUDGET AIRLINES

Milan is served by several budget airlines.

**British Midland** www.iflybritishmidland.com
**Easyjet** www.go-fly.com
**Ryanair** www.ryanair.com
**SkyEurope** www.skyeurope.com

### WEB FARES

There are many agencies offering travel on the web. The best include:

**Mobissimo** www.mobissimo.com
**Expedia** www.expedia.com
**Travelocity** www.travelocity.com

## BY TRAIN

Information about the Italian Railways (Trenitalia) can be obtained in the UK from European Rail Travel Ltd, 020 7387 0444, www.raileurope.co.uk. For direct information and tickets check www.trenitalia.it. Trenitalia Help Desk: +39 06 8833 9537, helpdesk@sipax.com.

In North America, Trenitalia information and tickets can be obtained from European Rail Travel, (877) 257 2887 in the US and 1-800-361-RAIL in Canada, or www.raileurope.com.

# GETTING TO THE CITY CENTRE

Linate Airport is connected to the city centre by Bus 73, which runs every 10 minutes from the arrivals terminal to near the underground station of San Babila on line M1 (Map 9, 1B). The journey takes 20 minutes, and tickets can be bought in the terminal for €1. There is also an express coach service between the airport and Milan Central Station. The bus terminal is on Piazza Luigi di Savoia (Map p. 84, 2B), and there is easy access to the underground station of Centrale on lines M1 and M3. Journey time is 30 minutes and tickets are €2.

Malpensa Airport is linked by a fast train, the Malpensa Express, to Cadorna Ferrovie Nord Station (underground line M1). The journey takes 50 minutes and tickets cost €9 (www.malpensaexpress.it). You also have a choice between two express coach lines: Air Pullman (departures every 20 minutes, journey time 60 minutes, tickets €4.50, 02 5858 3202, www.airpullman.com) and Malpensa Bus Express (departures every 20 minutes, journey time 60 minutes, tickets €5.50, 02 5858 3202, www.autostradale.com). They will drop you near the Trade Fair or at the Central Station (Piazza Luigi di Savoia, underground lines M2 and M3).

Orio al Serio Airport is connected to Milan by express coach services to Milan Central Station (underground lines M2 and M3). Journey time is 60 minutes, tickets are €3.35 (02 3391 0794, www.autostradale.com). There is also a service to Milan Lambrate Station (underground line M2). Journey time is 50 minutes, tickets are €6 (02 7060 3685, www.zaniviaggi.it).

Taxis are available at the terminal exits of all three airports.

# GETTING AROUND
## BY PUBLIC TRANSPORT

The underground lines, buses and trams run by ATM are very efficient. Public transport runs from approximately 6 am until midnight, and there is a bus service that replaces Line 1 of the underground at night.

For a metro map, turn to the inside back cover of this book.

### USEFUL TRAM AND BUS LINES

**1** Milano Centrale railway station—Piazza Cavour—Piazza Scala—Largo Cairoli (for the Castello Sforzesco)—Milano Nord railway station—Corso Sempione

**4** Piazza Repubblica—Via Manzoni—Piazza Scala—Via Legnano—Via Farini

**24** Via Mazzini—Corso Magenta (Santa Maria delle Grazie and Leonardo's *Last Supper*)

**19** Corso Sempione—Milano Nord railway station—Via Broletto—Via Orefici (for the Duomo)—Via Torino

**50, 54** Largo Augusto (duomo)—Corso Magenta—Via Carducci (for Sant'Ambrogio)—Via San Vittore

**61** Corso Matteotti—Piazza Scala—Via Brera—Via Solferino

**65** Milano Centrale railway station—Via San Gregorio—Corso Buenos Aires—Corso Venezia—Piazza Fontana—Via Larga—Corso Italia—Porta Lodovico

## TICKETS AND FARES

Tourist passes that last 24 and 48 hours and cost €3 and €5.50 respectively may be bought from newsstands in underground stations and from APT tourist information offices. Regular tickets cost €1 and are valid for 75 minutes on all forms of public transport, although they cannot be used twice on the underground. Tickets can be bought from newsstands, bars, tobacconists and automatic vending machines—but not on buses. Passengers must stamp their tickets when they get on a bus or tram, or at the turnstile in underground stations.

# BY CAR

It's not a good idea to use a car in Milan, as traffic is heavy in the centre of Milan and parking is restricted at all times. It's best to park in a supervised, pay car park, though with a bit of effort it is almost always possible to find a place to park free of charge away from the town centre. There are free car parks by the underground stations of Pagano (M1) and Lambrate (M2), and pay car parks at Rogoredo (M3) and Romolo (M2).

## PARKING IN THE CITY CENTRE

Vehicles that display a Sosta Milano card on the dashboard or rearview mirror are allowed to park ed in the areas marked by a blue line. Only residents may park in the areas marked by yellow lines.

Sosta Milano cards can be purchased from authorised ATM (Milan's transport company) retailers (usually tobacconists, bars and newsstands) and from ATM personnel (in uniform) near the parking areas. One hour in Zone A (city centre within the first ring of boulevards) will set you back €1.50 euro; two hours is €2. On Sundays, holidays and weekdays after 7 pm parking costs €2. In Zone B (outside the first ring of boulevards), one hour costs €1.20. If your vehicle is towed, contact the Municipal Police on 02 772 7232.

## BY TAXI

These are hired from ranks or by telephone (02 4040; 02 8383; 02 8585); there are no cruising cabs. Before taking a taxi it is advisable to make sure it has a meter in working order.

No tip is expected, but supplements are charged after 9 pm and for luggage. There is a heavy surcharge when the destination is outside the city limits (ask before you go how much the fare is likely to be).

## CAR HIRE

Arrangements for car hire can be made before departure through the airlines (at advantageous rates as part of package deals) or in Italy through any of the principal car hire firms (the best known include Maggiore, Avis and Hertz), which offer daily, five-day, weekly and weekend rates. Special rates are available for periods of 30 days and over.

## CURRENCY

In Italy, the monetary unit is the euro (€), and has been currency for daily use since 2002. There are banks with ATMs accepting Visa and MasterCard, Maestro and Cirrus cards throughout the city, and most credit cards are now generally accepted in hotels, shops and restaurants.

Cash can be changed at banks, post offices, travel agencies and some hotels, restaurants and shops, though the rate of exchange can vary considerably from place to place. Banks are open Mon–Fri, 8.30 am–1.30 pm and 2.30 pm–4 pm, and are closed on Saturday, Sunday and public holidays. Afternoon opening hours may vary from bank to bank, and many banks close early (about 11 am) on days preceding national holidays.

Exchange offices are usually open seven days a week at airports and most main railway stations. A limited amount of euros can be obtained from conductors on international trains and at certain stations. For small amounts of money, the difference between hotel and bank rates may be negligible, as banks tend to take a fixed commission on transactions.

You can no longer exchange your old lire for euros, so any money you have left over from previous trips will have to remain a souvenir.

## WEB RESOURCES

The official website of the Milan tourist office (Azienda di Promozione Turistica del Milanese) is *www.milanoinfotourist.com*.

## GENERAL

Hello Milano, *www.hellomilano.it*. A general-info English site for visitors and residents.

## TRANSPORT

Azienda Trasporti Milanesi The official website for Milan's public transport system is *www.atm-mi.it*.

## INFORMATION OFFICES AND PUBLICATIONS

The Azienda di Promozione Turistica del Milanese (APT) provides information about hotel accommodation, railway and motorway connections, airlines and consulate addresses. It also provides opening times and acts as a box office.

The office also distributes city maps, hotel directories and a monthly entertainment magazine.

There are three main offices:

· Via Marconi 1, Map p. 8, 3C. 02 725 241, 02 7252 4350
  Stazione Centrale, Map. p. 84, 2B, underground line M1. 02 7252 4360
  Corso Venezia 43, Map p. 9, 2B. 02 77451.

## MILAN WELCOME CARD

APT offices also sells the Milan Welcome Card, which gives discounts on museum admissions and public transport. It also offers deals on city tours, guided visits to exhibitions and art galleries, and excursions (including a boat trip along the Naviglio Grande).

## TAX REBATES

If you're a non-EU resident, you can claim VAT rebates on purchases made in Italy, provided the total expenditure is more than €150. Ask the vendor for a receipt describing the goods acquired and get it checked and stamped by Italian customs on leaving Italy (take extra time for this). Then send the vendor back the receipt when you get home, within 90 days of purchase. The vendor will forward the tax rebate (currently 20% on most goods) to your home address.

## TELEPHONE AND POSTAL SERVICES

Stamps are sold at tobacconists (*tabacchi*) and post offices. Correspondence can be addressed c/o the post office by adding '*Fermo Posta*' to the name of the locality.

For all calls in Italy, local and long-distance, dial the area code (for instance, 080 for Bari), then the telephone number. For international and intercontinental calls, dial 00 plus the country code, then the area code.

Florence area code 02
Dialling UK from Italy (0044)+ number without the initial zero
Dialling US from Italy (001) + number
Dialling Milan from UK (0039) + number
Dialling Milan from US (011 39) + number

You can reach an AT&T operator at 800-172-444, MCI at 800-90-5825, or Sprint at 800-172-405. For directory assistance call 12 (for numbers in Italy) or 176 (for international numbers). You can receive a wake-up call on your phone by dialling 114 and following the prompts (in Italian).

## INTERNET CENTRES

**Fnac Cafè** Via Torino, corner of Via della Palla **Map 99, 2B**

**Gr@zia Internet Cafè Duca d'Aosta** Piazza Duca d'Aosta 14 (by Stazione Centrale) **Map p. 84, 2B**

## HEALTH AND INSURANCE

British citizens, as members of the EU, can claim for health treatment in Italy if they have an E111 form (issued by the DSS). There are also a number of private holiday health insurance policies. Italy has no medical programme covering US or Canadian citizens, who are advised to take out an insurance policy before travelling.

# EMERGENCIES AND PERSONAL SECURITY

**Police** 113 (Polizia di Stato) or 112 (Carabinieri)

**Fire brigade** 115

**Medical emergencies** 118

**Lost or stolen credit cards** American Express 055 238 2876; Mastercard 800 872 050; Visa 800 877 232

**Road assistance** 116

**Towed cars** 02 77271

Pickpocketing is a widespread problem in towns all over Italy, and it is always advisable not to carry valuables in your pocket and to be particularly careful on public transport. Never wear conspicuous jewellery, including necklaces and expensive watches; women, when walking, should keep their bags on the side of their bodies away from the road. Crime should be reported at once to the police. A detailed statement has to be given in order to get an official document confirming loss or damage (essential for insurance claims). Interpreters are provided.

## EMBASSIES AND CONSULATES

**Australia** Via Borgogna 2, 02 777041; Mon–Fri, 9 am–12 pm, 2 pm–4 pm **Map p. 8, 1B**

**Canada** Via Vittor Pisani 19, 02 67581; Mon–Thur, 8.30 am–12.30 pm, 13.15 pm–5.30 pm; Fri 8.30 am–1 pm **Map p. 84, 3C**

**Netherlands** Via San Vittore 45, 02 485 5841; Mon–Fri 9.30 am–12 pm; Tues and Thur, 1.30 pm–3.30 pm **Map p. 98, 1B**

**United Kingdom** Via San Paolo 7, 02 723001; Mon–Fri, 9.15 am–12.15 pm, 2.30 pm–4.30 pm **Map p. 8, 3B**

**United States** Via Prinipe Amedeo 2/10, 02 290351; Mon–Fri 9 am–12.30 pm, 2 pm–3.30 pm **Map p. 85, 2C**

## HEALTH AND MEDICAL SERVICES

**The Milan Clinic** Via Cerva 25. 02 7601 6047, www.milanclinic.com. The clinic, with English-speaking doctors trained in the UK and US, is open 9 am–7 pm, Mon–Fri, and is closed August between Christmas and January 6. **Map p. 9, 1C**

## DISABLED TRAVELLERS

All new public buildings are obliged by law to provide easy access and specially designed facilities for the disabled. Unfortunately, the conversion of historic buildings, including many museums and monuments, is made problematic by structural impediments such as narrow pavements. Barriers therefore continue to exist in many cases. Hotels that are equipped to accommodate the disabled are indicated in an annual list of hotels published by the tourist board. Airports and railway stations provide assistance and certain trains are equipped to transport wheelchairs. For further information, contact an APT office (see p. 157).

## FOOD AND DRINK

### THE CUISINE OF LOMBARDY

Milan is the capital of Lombardy, and although Lombardy is the most prosperous region of Italy, its many industries represent only half of its wealth: the other half comes from farming. The biggest aspect of that is livestock—mainly beef and dairy cattle, but also pigs, sheep and goats. Lombard cuisine therefore is characterised by abundant meat and cheese, and by the use of butter rather than olive oil in the preparation of traditional dishes.

The tastiest appetisers are *bresaola* (salted, air-dried beef sliced thin and served with olive oil, lemon and pepper), and *cicc* (a thin focaccia made with buckwheat polenta and cheese, fried in lard), both from the alpine Valtellina.

Good first courses are the ravioli, typical of Bergamo and Brescia, known as *casonei* (made with *salame*, spinach, egg, raisins, amaretti, cheese and breadcrumbs, served in a butter and sage sauce); the characteristically yellow *risotto alla milanese* (rice toasted with butter, onion and beef marrow, then cooked in meat broth with saffron); *pizzoccheri* from the Valtellina (ribbons of buckwheat pasta boiled together with potatoes and vegetables and dressed with a sauce of sautéed garlic, butter and bitto cheese); and the Mantuan *tortelli di zucca* (large tortellini filled with amaretti, pumpkin, egg, spiced apples and parmesan cheese, usually served in a butter and cheese sauce).

As a main course, try *cotoletta alla milanese* (a breaded veal cutlet fried in butter, appropriated by Milan's former occupiers, the Austrians, and renamed Wiener Schnitzel); *osso buco*, another Milanese dish (sliced veal shin cooked slowly in tomato sauce and *gremolada*, a mixture of lemon zest, rosemary, sage and parsley, usually served with rice); or *lavarelli al vino bianco* (a fresh-water fish from the Lombard lakes sautéed in butter, parsley and white wine).

An interesting local *contorno* (usually served with boiled meats) is *mostarda di Cremona* (a fruit compote made with honey and white wine and seasoned with mustard and other spices).

Good desserts include the Milanese Christmas cake panettone (made with flour, natural leavening, butter, sugar, egg, candied fruit and raisins); *polenta dolce* (cornflour cooked with milk, egg yolks, amaretti, butter and cinnamon); and Mantuan *torta sbrisolona* (wheat and cornflour, sugar, egg yolks, chopped almonds, baked until dry then crumbled rather than sliced).

Lombardy has one DOCG wine (*Denominazione di Origine Controllata e Garantita*, the hightest controlled and limited category) and 15 DOC (*Denominazione di Origine Controllata*, the second-highest category) wines.

Franciacorta, is the most famous and important (as well as the most expensive). It is vinified red, white, rosé and sparkling. Franciacorta red is made from Cabernet Franc and Cabernet Sauvignon grapes blended with Barbera, Nebbiolo and Merlot. Franciacorta white is Chardonnay and Pinot Bianco.

Probably the most interesting Lombard wines are the Valtellina reds, made from Nebbiolo grapes, here called Chiavennasca, by small 'boutique' growers. The spectacular vineyards of the Valtellina cling like moss to the rocks of this steep Alpine valley, in terraces at altitudes as high as 800 m. The DOCs Valtellina and Valtellina Superiore are divided into four sub-appellations: Grumello, Inferno, Sassella and Valgella, all delicious with red and white meat. Late-pressed (forced) grapes make the rich, strong (16%) and very special Sfurzat.

Also interesting in Lombardy are the Lake Garda wines, which offer outstanding quality at a relatively low price, and the table wines of the Oltrepò Pavese (the area south of the Po, bordering on Emilia-Romagna), fragrant whites and full-bodied reds, some of which are surprisingly smooth and complex.

## RESTAURANTS

Italian restaurants are usually good and inexpensive. Generally speaking, the least pretentious *ristorante* (restaurant), *trattoria* (small restaurant) or *osteria* (inn or tavern) provides the best value. The restaurants listed in each chapter have been chosen for the quality and distinction of their cuisine and the extent of their wine lists; even the simplest are quite good. Like hotels, they have been rated by price: consider an expensive (€€€) meal one that will cost you €45 or more, a moderate (€€) meal

€20-45, and an inexpensive (€) meal under €20. As a rule, the more exclusive eateries are considerably cheaper at midday. You should telephone and make a reservation, as all the establishments listed provide good value for money and are likely to be very popular.

Prices on the menu do not include the cover charge (shown separately, usually at the bottom of the page). The service charge (*servizio*) is sometimes automatically added at the end of the bill, and if it is, tipping is not strictly necessary, but is appreciated. Many simpler establishments do not offer a written menu, and here, although the choice is limited, the standard of cuisine is usually quite acceptable.

## WINE BARS

Wine bars provide a good alternative to restaurants for a quick lunch or a mid-afternoon snack. They are also a good place to meet friends in the evening. Most offer a daily selection of wines of varying price, plus light meals.

## CAFÉS

Cafés are open from early morning to late at night and serve all sorts of excellent refreshments that are usually eaten standing up. As a rule, you must pay the cashier first, then present your receipt to the barman in order to get served. If you sit at a table the charge is usually higher and you will be given waiter service, and don't have to pay first.

*Caffè* (that is, a shot of espresso) can be ordered *lungo* (diluted), *corretto* (with a liqueur) or *macchiato* (with a dash of hot milk). A cappuccino is an espresso with more hot milk than a *caffè macchiato* and is generally considered a breakfast drink. A glass of hot milk with a dash of coffee in it, called *latte macchiato*, is another early-morning favourite. In summer, many drink *caffè freddo* (iced coffee).

## OPENING TIMES

### GALLERIES, MUSEUMS AND CHURCHES

The opening times of museums and monuments have been given in the text, but they often change without warning. The tourist board keeps updated timetables of most museums. National museums and monuments are usually open daily 8.15 am–6.50 pm, plus evening hours in summer. Churches open quite early in the morning (often for 6 am

Mass), but are normally closed for a considerable period during the middle of the day (from around 12 pm to around 4 pm). Some churches now ask that sightseers do not enter during a service, but normally visitors may do so, provided they are silent and do not approach the altar in use. At all times they are expected to cover their legs and arms, and generally dress with decorum. In Holy Week most of the pictures are covered.

## SHOPS
Shops are generally open Mon–Sat, from around 9 am–1 pm and around 4 pm–8 pm. Shops selling clothes and other goods are usually closed on Monday morning and food shops on Wednesday afternoon. This changes from mid-June to mid-September, when all shops are closed instead on Saturday afternoon.

## PUBLIC HOLIDAYS

  1 January
25 April (Liberation Day)
    Easter Sunday and Easter Monday
  1 May (Labour Day)
24 June (St John the Baptist, patron saint)
15 August (Assumption)
  1 November (All Saints' Day)
  8 December (Immaculate Conception)
25 December (Christmas Day)
26 December (St Stephen)

## TIME
Italy is one hour ahead of Greenwich Mean Time and six hours ahead of Eastern Standard Time in the US. Daylight saving time in Italy usually runs from April to October.

## TIPPING
A service charge of 15%–18% is added to hotel bills, usually already part of the inclusive price of your room. Still, it is customary to leave an additional tip in any case. Depending on the category of your hotel, a tip

of €1–2 is suggested for any hotel staff except the concierge, who may expect €2-3.

Restaurants add a service charge of approximately 15% to all bills. It is customary, however, to leave a small tip (5%–10%) for good service. In cafés and bars, leave 15% if you sit at a table (unless the bill already includes service) and 10–20 euro cents if standing at a counter or bar to drink. At the theatre, opera and concerts, tip ushers 50 cents or more, depending on the price of your seat.

## WEIGHTS AND MEASURES

Italians use the metric system of weights and measures. The *metro* is the unit of length, the *grammo* of weight, the *ara* of land and the *litro* of capacity. Greek-derived prefixes (*deca-*, *etto-*, *chilo-*) are used with those names to express multiples; Latin prefixes (*deci-*, *centi-*, *milli*) to express fractions (1 *chilometro*=1,000 *metri*, while a *millimetro*=1,000th part of a *metro*). For approximate calculations, the *metro* may be taken as 39 inches and the *chilometro* as 0.6 miles; the *litro* as 1.75 pints; an *etto* as 3.5 oz; and the *chilo* as 2.2 lb.

## PLACES TO STAY

The hotels listed, regardless of their cost, have been chosen on the basis of their character or location. All have something special about them— beautiful surroundings or a distinctive atmosphere—and even the humblest are comfortable. Generally speaking, you should expect a double room at an expensive (€€€) hotel to cost €200 or more, a moderate (€€) hotel to cost €100-200 and an inexpensive (€) hotel to cost under €100. The local tourist offices will help you find  accommodation on the spot, but that's taking a big risk if you're travelling in the high season or during one of Milan's many trade fairs. You should try to book well in advance, especially if you're planning to travel between May and October. Hotels will allow you to claim back part or all of your deposit if you cancel the booking at least 72 hours in advance. Hotels equipped to offer hospitality to the disabled are indicated in the tourist boards' hotel lists.

In all hotels the service charges are included in the rates and the total charge is exhibited on the back of the hotel room door. Breakfast is by law an optional extra charge, although a lot of hotels try to include it in the price of the room. When booking a room, always specify if you want breakfast or not—it is usually more fun (and cheaper) to go around the corner to the nearest café for breakfast. Hotels are now obliged by law (for tax purposes) to issue an official receipt to customers and you should not leave the premises without this document.

## THE CITY CENTRE

€€ **Gran Duca di York** Via Moneta 1a, 02 874863, fax 02 869 0344. A comfortable hotel in a carefully restored early 19th-C townhouse. **Map p. 8, 1C**

**Manzoni** Via Santo Spirito 20, 02 7600 5700, fax 02 784212 , www.hotelmanzoni.com. Quiet, comfortable and popular, in the heart of the shopping district. Book in advance. **Map p. 9, 1A**

**Spadari al Duomo** Via Spadari 11, 02 7200 2371, fax 02 861184, www.spadarihot.com. Beautiful rooms and an interesting collection of contemporary art contribute to the elegant atmosphere of this recent establishment, just a few paces away from the Duomo. Closed in Dec. **Map p. 8, 2C**

€€€ **Brunelleschi** Via Baracchini 12, 02 8843, fax 02 870144, www.milanhotel.it. An elegant modern creation in the heart of the historic centre. **Map p. 8, 3C**

**Carlton Baglioni** Via Senato 5, 02 77077, fax 02 78330, www.baglionihotels.com. Modern and comfortable, on the edge of the historic city centre. **Map p. 9, 1B**

**De la Ville** Via Hoepli 6, 02 867651, fax 02 866609, www.sinahotels.it. Comfortable and strategically located between the cathedral, La Scala and the shopping district. **Map p. 8, 3B**

**Four Seasons** Via Gesù 8, 02 77088, fax 02 7708 5000, www.fourseasons.com. The usual high standard of luxury offered by this international group in a beautifully restored convent in the shopping district. **Map p. 8, 3B**

**Grand Hotel Duomo** Via San Raffaele 1, 02 8833, fax 02 864 62027, www.grandhotelduomo.com. Refined elegance and a unique position, so close to the cathedral you can almost reach out and touch it from the rooms and terraces. **Map p. 8, 3C**

**Grand Hotel et de Milan** Via Manzoni 29, 02 723141, fax 02 8646 086, www.grandhoteletdemilan.it. Milan's finest for over 130 years, in a centrally located, tastefully renovated patrician palace. **Map p. 8, 3A**

**Sir Edward** Via Mazzini 4, 02 877877, fax 02 877844, www.hotelsiredward.it. A refined establishment with 38 rooms, on the edge of the shopping district. **Map p. 8, 2C**

## BRERA

€    **Antica Locanda Solferino** Via Castelfidardo 2, 02 657 0129, fax 02 657 1361, www.anticalocandasolferino.it. in the heart of the Brera district, Milan's 'left bank', with a wide following of return clients—book well in advance. **Map p. 53, 1B**

€€   **Antica Lodanda dei Mercanti** Via San Tomaso 6, 02 805 4080, fax 02 805 4090, www.locanda.it. A small, cosy hotel with elegant rooms of various size and shape, some with terrace and rooftop views. No restaurant. **Map p. 52, 3C**

**Regency** Via Arimondi 12, 02 3921 6021, fax 02 3921 7734, www.regency-milano.com. Off the map: behind Parco Sempione. A charming, refined hotel in a 19th-C aristocratic townhouse with a beautiful courtyard and working fireplace in winter. A long walk from the city centre, no restaurant. Closed in Dec-Jan and in Aug.

## PORTA VENEZIA

€€   **Sanpi** Via Lazzaro Palazzi 18, 02 2951 3341, fax 02 2940 2451, www.hotelsanpimilano.it. In a modern building with a small garden, good attention to detail. Closed in Dec and Aug. **Map p. 85, 1B**

€€€**Manin** Via Manin 7, 02 659 6511, fax 02 655 2160, www.hotel manin.it. Central, quiet and comfortable, overlooking the Giardini Pubblici. **Map p. 85, 2C**

**Principe di Savoia** Piazza della Repubblica 17, 02 62301, fax 02 659 5838, www.principedisavoia.com. A luxury hotel popular with Americans, in a shady square midway between the Stazione Centrale and the historic city centre. **Map p. 85, 1C**

**Sheraton Diana Majestic** Viale Piave 42, 02 20581, fax 02 2058 2058, www.starwood.com. Early-20th-C atmosphere and style and modern comfort in a recently renovated building. **Map p. 85, 2B**

## SANT'AMBROGIO

€€   **Antica Locanda Leonardo** Corso Magenta 78, 02 4801 4197, fax 02 4801 9012, www.leoloc.com. A luxury atmosphere but family-style friendliness in a hotel overlooking a small inner court, near the Church of Santa Maria delle Grazie. No restaurant. Closed in Dec-Jan and in Aug. **Map p. 98, 1B**

**Mini Hotel Tiziano** Via Tiziano 6, 02 469 9035, 02 481 2153, www.minihot.it. Off the map, east of Parco Sempione. Near the Trade Fair, outside the historic centre, with comfortable rooms and a small garden.

**Regina** Via Cesare Correnti 13, 02 5810 6913, fax 02 5810 7033, www.hotelregina.it. Modern interior décor, parquet floors and well-appointed rooms in an 18th-C building. No restaurant. Closed in Dec-Jan and in Aug. **Map p. 98, 3C**

**Rubens** Via Rubens 21, 02 40302, fax 02 48193114, www.antareshotels.com. Off the map, east of Parco Sempione. Near the Trade Fair, outside the historic centre. A quietly elegant place, well thought-out in every detail, with paintings by contemporary artists.

**€€€Pierre Milano** Via De Amicis 32, 02 7200 0581, fax 02 805 2157 www.hotelpierremilano.it. Quiet and atmospheric, in the historic city centre near the church of Sant'Ambrogio. **Map p. 98, 2C**

## NAVIGLI

**€€ Dei Cavalieri** Piazza Missori 1, 02 88571, fax 02 7202 1683, www.hoteldeicavaliei.com. Small public areas, but comfortable rooms and a fine terrace. **Map p. 123, 1A**

**Mercure Corso Genova** Via Conca del Naviglio 20, 02 5810 4141, fax 02 8940 1012, www.mercure.com. comfortable and centrally located, between Sant'Ambrogio and San Lorenzo. **Map p. 122, 2B**

## BED AND BREAKFAST

B&B accommodation, usually in private homes and villas, may be booked through a central agency. Try **Caffelletto** at www.caffelletto.it or check **BedandBreakfast.Com** at www.bedandbreakfast.com or **Bed & Breakfast in Europe** at www.bedandbreakfastineurope.com/italia.

# art glossary

**Alessi, Galeazzo** (c. 1512–72). Genoese architect and sculptor who imported Mannerist and Baroque ideas from Rome to Milan.

**Balla, Giacomo** (1871-1958). Italian artist and founding member of the **Futurist** movement in painting.

**Bambaia, Il** (Agostino Busti: 1483–1548). Sculptor of the Lombard school whose most famous work is the *Tomb of Gaston de Foix* (1515–22) in the Museo di Arte Antica at Castello Sforzesco (see p. 67). Gaston de Foix was a French hero and the nephew of Louis XII; he died in the Battle of Ravenna in 1512. He controlled Milan briefly with Gian Giacomo Trivulzio in 1511.

**Barocci, Federico** (1526–1612). A 16th-C central Italian painter and an important precursor of the Baroque style. Barocci was born in Urbino and, apart from two trips to Rome, remained there all his life. His paintings show stylistic debts to **Raphael** and Correggio, and are seen as the *trait d'union* between the High Renaissance masters of the 16th C and the new art that was to emerge in the next century. He is said to have abandoned his frescoes in the Casino of Pius IV in the Vatican Gardens (1561–63) for fear that his rivals were trying to poison him.

**Baroque** A style in the Western arts roughly coinciding with the 17th C, though early manifestations in Italy occur in the late 16th C. Baroque painting and sculpture are distinguished by the desire to evoke emotional states by appealing to the senses, often in dramatic ways. Some of the qualities most frequently associated with the Baroque are grandeur, sensuous richness, drama, vitality, movement, tension, emotional exuberance, and a tendency to blur distinctions between the various arts.

**Bellini, Giovanni** (1430–1516). The leading figure of the early Renaissance in Venice. His style shows a steady evolution from purely religious, narrative emphasis to a new naturalism of. setting and landscape.The *Pietà*, *Madonna Greca* and *Madonna and Child* in a landscape, in the Brera Gallery (see p. 54), and the *Pietà* in the Museo Poldi Pezzoli (see p. 20) are brilliant examples of his masterful command of colour. Jacopo Bellini, his father, and Gentile, his brother, also are important Venetian Renaissance painters.

**Bergognone, Ambrogio** (da Fossano, active 1480–1522). Lombard Renaissance painter known especially for his paintings of the Virgin, modelled on those of **Vincenzo Foppa** and **Leonardo da Vinci**, his masters. His use of subtle, subdued colours won him the nickname, 'Whistler of the Renaissance'. Together with Foppa he is considered the greatest painter of the Milanese school. His panel paintings may be seen at in the Brera Gallery (see p. 54) and the Ambrosiana (see p. 124); his frescoes, in the church of San Simpliciano (see p. 73).

**Boccioni, Umberto** (1882–1916). Italian painter, sculptor and theorist of the Futurist movement, killed in action in World War I. See picture on p. 120.

**Boltraffio, Giovanni Antonio** (1457–1516). Milanese Renaissance painter and pupil of Leonardo da Vinci. *The Lady in Red* in the Pinacoteca di Brera (see p. 54) is one of his better-known portraits.

**Bordone, Paris** (1500–1570). An aristocrat who studied under Titian for several years, and then Giorgione. He was so strongly influenced by Titian that, over the years, works by Bordone have been attributed to the teacher. Notable works in Milan include a *Baptism of Christ* in the Brera (see p. 59).

**Botticelli, Sandro** (1445–1510). Alessandro Di Mariano Filipepi. This superlative artist's earlier compositions are imbued with Humanist literary and philosophical references, whereas his later works evince a deep sense of Christian piety. His *Pietà* and *Madonna* in the Museo Poldi Pezzoli (see p. 19 and picture on p. 21) and his tondo of the *Madonna and Child* in the Pinacoteca Ambrosiana (see p. 127) are among his more lyrical works.

**Bramante, Donato** (1444–1514). Bramante was the greatest architect of the High Renaissance, and an accomplished painter, as well. His early works in Milan included the rectory of Sant'Ambrogio (p. 100) and the church of Santa Maria delle Grazie (p. 108). In Rome, Bramante served as principal planner for Pope

Julius II's project to rebuild the city. His only known panel painting, showing Christ at the column, is in the Pinacoteca di Brera (see p. 61).

**Caravaggio** (1571?–1610). Michelangelo Merisi. This Lombard painter's revolutionary technique of dramatic, selective illumination of form out of deep shadow became a hallmark of Baroque painting. Scorning the traditional idealized interpretation of religious subjects, he took his models from the streets and painted them realistically. The *Supper at Emmaus*, in the Pinacoteca di Brera (p. 62), and *Basket of Fruit*, in the Pinacoteca Ambrosiana (see p. 127 and picture on p. 128), are among the artist's best-known masterpieces.

**Carrà, Carlo** (1881–1966). One of the more influential Italian painters of the first half of the 20th C, best known for his **Futurist** and **Metaphysical** paintings. Carrà studied at the Brera Academy of Art.

**Carriera, Rosalba** (1675–1757). Venetian portrait painter and miniaturist, who was also active in Paris (1720–21) and Vienna (1730). Best known for her work in pastels, she was an originator of the Rococo style in Italy and France.

**Classicism** and **Neo-Classicism** Historical tradition or aesthetic attitudes based on the art of ancient Greece and Rome in antiquity. Classicism refers either to the art produced in antiquity or to later art inspired by it; Neo–Classicism always refers to the art produced later. Because of the efforts of 15th- and 16th-C Italians to absorb the Classicism of antiquity, the Italian Renaissance was the first period of thoroughgoing Classicism after antiquity. Leon Battista Alberti equated Classicism and beauty: 'the harmony and concord of all the parts achieved by following well-founded rules and resulting in a unity such that nothing could be added or taken away or altered except for the worse'. He said that the Classical sculptor should endeavour as much as possible to express the life and character of the subject through the deportment and bearing of the figure. In painting, artists were supposed to choose subjects that glorified man, use figures suited to the actions being represented, and imitate the appearance of actions in the natural world.

**Cossa, Francesco del** (c. 1438–c. 1481). Early Renaissance painter of the Ferrarese school who exercised a deep influence on northern Italian painting. The side panels of a polyptych by Cossa, which show Saints John the Baptist and Peter, are in the Pinacoteca di Brera (see p. 59). The polyptych originally included a central painting of St Vincent Ferrer and other elements now lost.

**Crespi, Daniele** (1590–1663). Milanese Baroque painter known for the direct emotional appeal and simple compositions of his religious paintings—elements much appreciated by the Counter Reformation. His portrait of *St Charles Borromeo at Supper* at the church of Santa Maria della Passione (see p. 25) is his best-known work.

**Crespi, Giuseppe Maria** (1665–1747). Bolognese Baroque painter who broke dramatically with the formal academic tradition to achieve a direct, immediate approach to his subject matter. Best known for his painter of pictures of everyday life, such as the *Village Fair* in the Pinacoteca di Brera (see p. 54), he also applied his innovative approach to religious paintings.

**Crivelli, Carlo** (1430/5–95). The earliest records devoted to this Venetian artist date from 1457, when he was sentenced to six months in jail for living with a sailor's wife. Upon his release he probably went to Padua, where he joined Francesco Squarcione's workshop; afterwards he worked in east-central Italy and in Dalmatia (now Croatia). The Brera *Madonna della Candaletta* (see p. 61) exemplifies the sumptuous drawing, refined rendering of different materials, and superfluity of decoration that characterised his mature style.

**Dyck, Sir Antony van** (1599–1641). One of the more prominent and prolific Flemish painters of the 17th C. After studying in the workshops of Hendrik van Balen and Peter Paul Rubens in Antwerp, he established a reputation as a painter of portraits of European aristocracy. He also executed many works on religious and mythological subjects and was a fine draftsman and etcher.

Appointed court painter by Charles I of England in 1632, he was knighted the same year.

**Ferrari, Gaudenzio** (1484–1546). Painter active in Piedmont and Lombardy, known for his original, powerful compositions. Though his early work was strongly influenced by **Leonardo** and his Milanese followers, throughout his life he remained an artist of considerable power and individuality. The detached fresco showing the *Annunciation to Joachim and Anna* in the Pinacoteca di Brera (see p. 54) is a late work (1544–45).

**Filarete** (c. 1400–69). Antonio di Pietro Averlino. Florentine architect, sculptor and writer, famous for his *Trattato d'Architettura* ('Treatise on Architecture'), which described plans for an ideal Renaissance city. He probably trained with Lorenzo Ghiberti, and his most important work in sculpture, the bronze doors of St Peter's in Rome (1433–45) are deeply indebted to Ghiberti's doors for the Baptistery in Florence. In 1451 he entered the service of Francesco Sforza, Duke of Milan, and worked mainly as an architect. His Ospedale Maggiore, or Ca' Granda, (1457–65, finished in the 18th C) is among the first Renaissance buildings in Lombardy (see p. 138).

**Foppa, Vincenzo** (active 1427–1515). A leading figure in 15th-C Lombard painting until the arrival of **Leonardo da Vinci** in Milan (in c. 1481). The frescoed scenes (1466–68) of the life of St Peter Martyr in the Cappella Portinari at Sant'Eustorgio (see p. 131), comprise the most important Renaissance fresco cycle in the city.

**Futurism** In Italian, *Futurismo*. Early 20th-C artistic movement that centred in Italy and emphasized the dynamism, speed, energy, and power of the machine, the vitality, change, and the restlessness of modern life in general. The best-known Futurist artists include **Umberto Boccioni** (see picture on p. 120), **Carlo Carrà**, Luigi Russolo, Giacomo Balla and **Gino Severini**.

**Gothic** A style of painting, sculpture and architecture that flourished in Europe during the Middle Ages. Gothic art evolved from Romanesque art and lasted roughly from the 13th to the 15th C in Florence. Architecture was the most important and original art form during the Gothic period. The principal structural elements of Gothic architecture are ribbed vaults and pointed (ogival or lancet) arches, which distribute thrust from heavy walls and ceilings in a highly efficient manner. These elements enabled Gothic masons to build much larger and taller buildings than their Romanesque predecessors and to give their structures more complicated ground plans.

The term Gothic was coined by Italian Renaissance writers who attributed the invention (and what to them was the non-Classical ugliness) of medieval architecture to the barbarian Goths that had destroyed the Roman Empire and its Classical culture. The term retained its derogatory overtones until the 19th C, at which time a positive critical revaluation of Gothic architecture took place.

**Hayez, Francesco** (1791–1881). Hayez was the chief exponent of Italian Romanticism, known especially for his sensitive portraits. His *Kiss*, at the Brera (see p. 62 and picture on p. 60), remains a favourite for its unabashed romanticism. Hayez, whose family wanted him to be a painting restorer, instead went on to success as a painter and a teacher at the Brera Academy of Art.

**Humanism** Although the spirit of the Renaissance ultimately took many forms, it was expressed earliest by the intellectual movement called Humanism. Humanism was initiated by secular men of letters, rather than by the scholar-clerics who had previously dominated medieval intellectual life. Its predecessors were people like Dante and Petrarch, and its chief protagonists included the Florentines Marsilio Ficino and Pico della Mirandola.

Humanism had several significant features. First, it took human nature in all of its various manifestations and achievements as its subject. Second, it stressed the unity and compatibility of the truth found in all philosophical and theological schools and systems, a doctrine known as syncretism. Third, it emphasized the dignity of man. In place of the medieval ideal of a life of penance as the highest and noblest form of human activity, the Humanists looked to the struggle of creation and the attempt to exert mastery over nature. Finally, Humanism looked forward to a rebirth of a lost human spirit and wisdom. In the course of striving to recover these lost values, however, the Humanists sparked a new spiritual and intellectual outlook and cultivated a new body of knowledge. The effect of Humanism was to help people break free from the mental strictures imposed by religious orthodoxy, to inspire free inquiry and criticism, and to inspire a new confidence in the possibilities of human thought and action.

**Lega, Silvestro** (1826–95). Lega was a leading member of the group of 19th-C Florentine and Neapolitan painters who reacted against the rule-bound Italian academies of art and looked to nature for instruction. His *Pergolato*, in the Pinacoteca di Brera (see p. 62), shows a clear debt to Corot and the French Impressionists.

**Leonardo** (1452–1519). Leonardo da Vinci. Painter, draftsman, sculptor, architect, and engineer: Leonardo, perhaps more than any other figure, epitomized the Renaissance Humanist ideal. The fame that Leonardo enjoyed in his lifetime and that, filtered by historical criticism, has remained undimmed to the present day rests largely on his unlimited desire for knowledge, which guided all his thinking and behaviour. *The Last Supper* in the Cenacolo of Santa Maria delle Grazie (see p. 109) is his only surviving mural painting and one of his highest achievements. In Milan he also designed the frecoed decoration in the vault of the Sala delle Asse at Castello Sforzesco (see p. 65(, and painted a small *Portrait of a Musician* now in the Pinacoteca Ambrosiana (see p. 127).

**Lotto, Lorenzo** (1480–1556). Late Renaissance painter known for his perceptive portraits and mystical paintings of religious subjects. In the earlier years of his life he lived at Treviso, and, although biographer Giorgio Vasari says he trained with Giorgione and **Titian** in the Venetian workshop of **Giovanni Bellini**, he always remained somewhat apart from the main Venetian tradition. His *Boy Holding a Book of Petrarch*, in the Civiche Raccolte d'Arte at Castello Sforzesco (see p. 63), is one of the more enigmatic works of Renaissance portraiture.

**Luini, Bernardino** (1475?–1532). Lombard Renaissance painter best known for his mythological and religious frescoes. Luini was the most prominent of **Leonardo da Vinci**'s followers in Lombardy and, although little is known of his life, his prolific output suggests he enjoyed a successful career. Leonardo's influence can be seen in the facial types and the composition of Luini's *Holy Family with St Anne and the Young St John* in the Pinacoteca Ambrosiana (see p. 125).

**Mannerism** The style and practice that predominated in Italy from the end of the High Renaissance in the 1520s to the beginnings of the Baroque age around 1590. Mannerism originated as a reaction to the harmonious Classicism and the idealized naturalism of High Renaissance art as practiced by **Leonardo** and **Michelangelo**. In the portrayal of the human nude the standards of formal complexity had been set by Michelangelo and the norm of idealized beauty by **Raphael**. But in the work of these artists' Mannerist successors, an obsession with style and technique in figural composition often outweighed the importance of subject matter. The highest value was placed upon the apparently effortless solution of intricate artistic problems, such as the portrayal of the nude in complex and artificial poses.

**Mantegna, Andrea** (1431?–1506). A painter and engraver, Andrea Mantegna was one of the foremost Italian painters of the 15th C and the first fully Renaissance artist of Northern Italy. He combined the Venetian school's command of colour and composition, with the interest in Classical art that reached Northern Italy from Florence. *Lamentation over the Dead Christ* in the Pinacoteca di Brera established him as a master of perspective and foreshortening (see p. 56 and picture on p. 58).

**Michelangelo** (1475–1564). Michelangelo di Lodovico Buonarroti Simoni. The Italian Renaissance sculptor, painter, architect, and poet who exerted an unequaled influence on the development of Western art. Michelangelo was considered the greatest living artist in his lifetime, and ever since then he has been held to be one of the more important artists of all times. A number of his works in painting, sculpture, and architecture rank among the most famous in existence. Although the frescoes on the ceiling of the Sistine Chapel are probably the best known of his works today, the artist thought of himself primarily as a sculptor. The *Rondanini Pietà*, in the Museo di Arte Antica at Castello Sforzesco, was the artist's last sculpture; it remained unfinished when he died (see p. 67).

**Morandi, Giorgio** (1890–1964). Painter and etcher whose simple, geometric still lifes of bottles, jars, and boxes were an important contribution to the development of 20th-C art. Drawing on sources as diverse as Piero della Francesca, Cézanne and Chardin, he devloped a withdrawn, meditative style.

**Piero Della Francesca** (1420–1492). A painter whose serene, disciplined exploration of perspective had little influence on his contemporaries but came to be recognized in the 20th C as a major contribution to the Italian Renaissance, Piero received his early training in Florence but spent the active part of his career in Urbino, Arezzo, Rimini, and his native Umbria. The *Montefeltro Altarpiece*, with the Madonna surrounded by angels and saints, is Piero's last known work. It hangs in the Pinacoteca di Brera (see p. 61).

**Pittura Metafisica** School of painting that flourished mainly between 1911 and 1920 in the works of the Italian artists Giorgio De Chirico, **Carlo Carrà** and **Giorgio Morandi**. The artists' intention was to use representational but bizarre and incongruous imagery—juxtaposing disparate objects set into deep perspectives—to disquiet the viewer. The movement had a strong influence on the Surrealists in the 1920s.

**Raphael** (1483–1520). Raffaello Sanzio. This master painter and architect of the Italian High Renaissance is best known for his Madonnas and for his large figure compositions in the Vatican in Rome, for which there is a cartoon in the Pinacoteca Ambrosiana (the *School of Athens*, the largest extant Renaissance drawing; see p. 127). His work is admired for its clarity of form and ease of composition and for its visual achievement of the Humanist ideal of human grandeur.

**Reni, Guido** (1575–1642). Early Italian Baroque painter noted for the classical idealism of his mythological and religious subjects. He strove toward a harmony in which reality is presented in idealized proportions. He admired the Renaissance balance of **Raphael**, but also the naturalism of **Caravaggio**. The mood of his paintings (for example, the *Saints Peter and Paul* in the Pinacoteca di Brera; see p. 61) is calm and serene, as are the studied softness of colour and form. His religious compositions made him one of the more famous painters of his day in Europe, and a model for other Italian Baroque artists.

**Renaissance** Literally 'rebirth', the term Renaissance refers to the period in European civilization immediately following the Middle Ages, conventionally held to have been characterized by a surge of interest in Classical learning and values. It was first used by French 18th-C art historians to describe theh reappearance of antique architectural forms on Italian buildings of the early 16th C. The Renaissance originated in Florence in the early 15th C and thence spread throughout Italy and Europe, gradually replacing the **Gothic** style of the late Middle Ages. It encouraged a revival of naturalism in painting and sculpture, and of **Classical** forms and ornament in architecture

**Romanesque** The name Romanesque refers to the fusion of Roman, Carolingian and Ottonian, Byzantine and Germanic traditions that characterised European art from around 1000 to about 1150. Although perhaps the most striking advances in Romanesque art were made in France, the style was current in all parts of Europe except those eastern areas that preserved a full–fledged Byzantine tradition. Its geographic distribution resulted in a wide variety of local types.

**Severini, Gino** (1883–1966). Painter whose synthesis of the styles of **Futurism** and Cubism was instrumental in gaining acceptance for the Futurist movement outside Italy.

**Signorelli, Luca** (c 1441–1523). Luca D'Egidio di Ventura de' Signorelli, also called Luca da Cortona. Renaissance painter, best known for his nudes and for his novel compositional devices.

**Sironi, Mario** (1885–1961). Italian painter and sculptor whose figural works and industrial cityscapes are among the the higher achievements of Novecento, the painting movement founded in Milan by critic Margherita Sarfatti and advocating a 'return to order' after the excesses of the early-20th-C avant gardes.

**Solari, Cristoforo** (1460–1527). Distinguished Italian sculptor and architect, brother and first teacher of **Andrea Solario**, the painter. He made several sculptures for the Duomo (see p. 10), and finished Bramante's cloister at Sant'Ambrogio (see p. 100).

**Solario, Andrea** (1473–1524). Lombard Renaissance painter, one of the more imporant followers of **Leonardo da Vinci**. His earliest dated work is the *Madonna and Child with Saints Joseph and Jerome* in the Pinacoteca di Brera (p. 54). *Portrait of a Man* in the same gallery (c. 1500) recalls the portrait style of Leonardo da Vinci.

**Tibaldi, Pellegrino** (1527–96). Chief architect of Milan's famous Duomo (see p. 10) after 1547. Although he is known principally as a painter and sculptor, he presided over the dedication of the cathedral and had an important role in designing its façade.

**Tiepolo, Giovanni Battista** (Giambattista) (1696-1770) The last of the great Venetian decorators, and arguably the greatest painter of the 18th C. He is known for his luminous, poetic frescoes, with figures and architecture receding into dizzy distances beyond the picture plane (Sant'Ambrogio frescoes, see p. 102).

**Tintoretto** (c. 1518–1594). Jacopo Robusti. A great **Mannerist** painter of the Venetian school and one of the more important artists of the late **Renaissance**. He is represented in Milan by several important paintings (*Infant Christ among the Doctors*, *Deposition*, and *Saints beneath the Cross*; *Finding of the Body of St Mark at Alexandria*) in the Pinacoteca di Brera (see p. 54).

**Titian** (1488/90–1576). Tiziano Vecellio. The greatest **Renaissance** painter of the Venetian school was recognized early in his own lifetime as an extraordinary painter, and his reputation has never suffered a decline. In 1590 the art theorist Giovanni Lomazzo declared him 'the sun amidst small stars not only among the Italians but all the painters of the world'. His famous painting of *St Jerome* is in the Pinacoteca di Brera (see p. 54).

# index

Photo editor: Hadley Kincade

Front cover: *Uomo che Scende dal Tram* by Achilles Funi, courtesy of the Civico Museo d'Arte Contemporanea, Milan. Photo by Fabio Saporetti. Back cover: Galleria Vittorio Emanuele II, photo by Cesare Cicardini

Permission to reproduce pictures throughout the book is: courtesy of the Milan Duomo (p. 14); with kind permission of Studio Italo Rota. Project: Arengario Museo del Novecento. Architects: Italo Rota with Emmanuele Auxilia, Paolo Montenari, Fabio Fornasari (p. 18); collection of G.G. Poldi Pezzoli, Museo Poldi Pezzoli, Milan, inv. 443 (p. 21); courtesy of Prada (p. 43); su concessione del Ministerio per i Beni e le Attivita Culturali (pp. 58, 60); Photo by Saverio Lombardi Vallauri, courtesy of Cosmit (p. 74); courtesy of Galleria Cardi (p. 77); Photo by Allesandro Russotti, courtesy of Cosmit (p. 78); courtesy The Project Gallery, New York and Kimsooja. Photo by Mario Tedeschi, 2004 (p. 89); courtesy of the Civico Museo d'Arte Contemporanea, Collezione Jucker, Milan. Photo by Fabio Saporetti (p. 120); ©Biblioteca Ambrosiana—Auth. No. INT 38/04 (p. 128); courtesy of the Museo Diocesano, Milan (p. 135)

Photographs by Cesare Cicardini (pp. 32, 38, 65, 93, 102, 104, 109, 113, 119, 133, 139, 140, 142); Monica Larner (p. 146); and Phil Robinson (p. 11, 119, 155).

art/shop/eat Milan

First edition 2005
Published by Blue Guides Limited, a Somerset Books company
The Studio, 51 Causton Street, London SWIP 4AT


ISBN 0-905131-03-8

© Paul Blanchard, 2005

Published in the United States of America by
WW Norton & Company, Inc
500 Fifth Avenue, New York, NY 10110, USA

ISBN 0-393-32784-1


Series devised by Gemma Davies

Layout and production: Anikó Kuzmich

Editor: Maya Mirsky
Consulting editor: Roberta Kedzierski
Copy editing: Mark Griffith

Floorplans by Imre Bába, ©Blue Guides Limited
Maps by Dimap Bt., ©Blue Guides Limited

Printed and bound in China by SunFung Offset Binding Co.,Ltd .

SOMERSET BOOKS

# art / shop / eat

art / shop / eat
## VENICE

art / shop / eat
## BERLIN

art / shop / eat
## MILAN

art / shop / eat
## FLORENCE

art / shop / eat
## LONDON

art / shop / eat
## NEW YORK

art / shop / eat
## ROME

art / shop / eat
## PARIS

art / shop / eat
## BARCELONA